Re___
and
Man

Our Story

Bassam:

Enjoy the read my friends

Leif

LEIF GUITEAU

outskirtspress
DENVER, COLORADO

The opinions expressed in this manuscript are solely the opinions of the author and do not represent the opinions or thoughts of the publisher. The author has represented and warranted full ownership and/or legal right to publish all the materials in this book.

Religion and Man
Our Story
All Rights Reserved.
Copyright © 2014 Leif Guiteau
v1.0

Cover Photo © 2014 Leif Guiteau. All rights reserved - used with permission.

This book may not be reproduced, transmitted, or stored in whole or in part by any means, including graphic, electronic, or mechanical without the express written consent of the publisher except in the case of brief quotations embodied in critical articles and reviews.

Outskirts Press, Inc.
http://www.outskirtspress.com

ISBN: 978-1-4787-3169-6

Outskirts Press and the "OP" logo are trademarks belonging to Outskirts Press, Inc.

PRINTED IN THE UNITED STATES OF AMERICA

Acknowledgements

I have to begin by thanking my mother Karen. She instilled in me a passion for learning at an early age. She helped nurture me in more ways than one, and I am so grateful to have her at my side. Her father, the late Rowland Budden, was also instrumental in giving me a strong appreciation for history. We had many long discussions on history and geopolitical events that fostered my views on the world and mankind's existence. My uncle, Dr. Jeff Budden, has also been like a father to me in recent years, I can't thank him enough. To Dr. Michael Budden, thank you for your assistance in composing my book, you were a tremendous asset. Also, LSU Baseball "superfan" Chris Guillot was a major inspiration for me. He barely knew me, but had the utmost faith in my ability to follow my dreams and compose this book. Chris reminded me of what LSU Baseball Hall of Fame Coach Skip Bertman would tell his players about the importance of visualization. You cannot achieve a goal without visualizing it first. What a tremendous tool that proved to be. Last, but certainly not least, I have to thank a former LSU batgirl for the baseball team, my wife Mary Mowad Guiteau. She has supported me through so much during hard times in my life. She has never wavered, always the steady presence by my side. I love her so much and do not know where I would be without her and our two wonderful children Carson and Layla. Thank you to everyone.....

Table of Contents

Maps i

Preface ix

Origins 1

Judaism 9

Christianity 24

Islam 37

Hinduism 48

Buddhism 57

China 66

Reflections 75

Maps

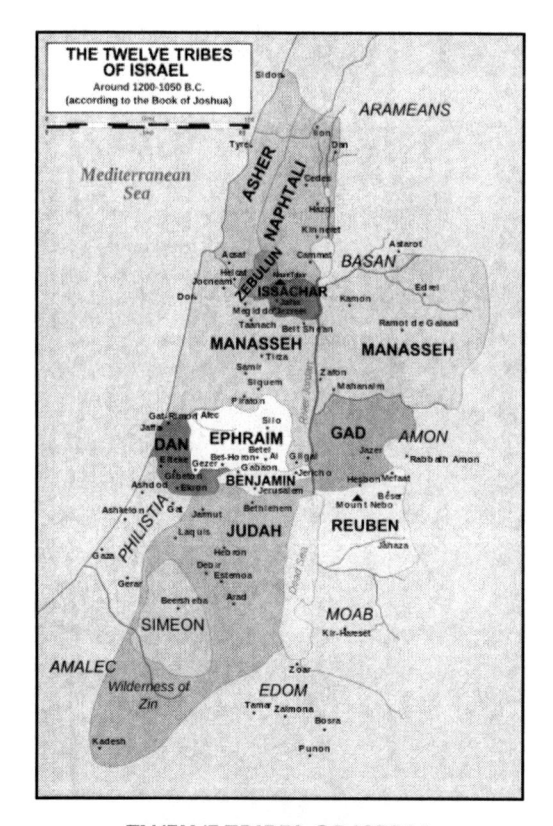

TWELVE TRIBES OF ISREAL

(Courtesy of Wikipedia)

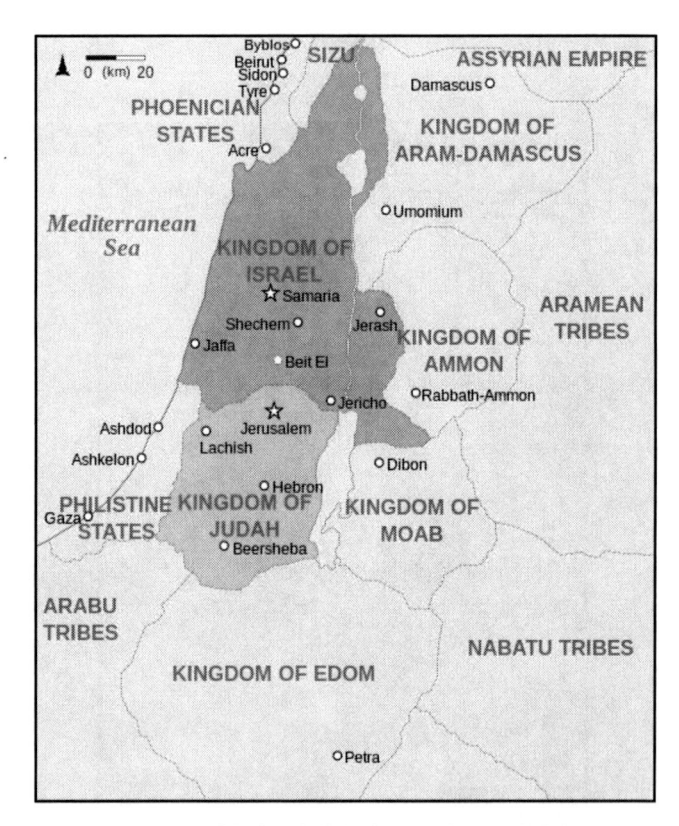

SPLIT KINGDOMS OF ISRAEL AND JUDAH
(Courtesy of Wikipedia)

ROMAN JUDAEA, 1ST CENTURY B.C.E.
(Courtesy of Wikipedia)

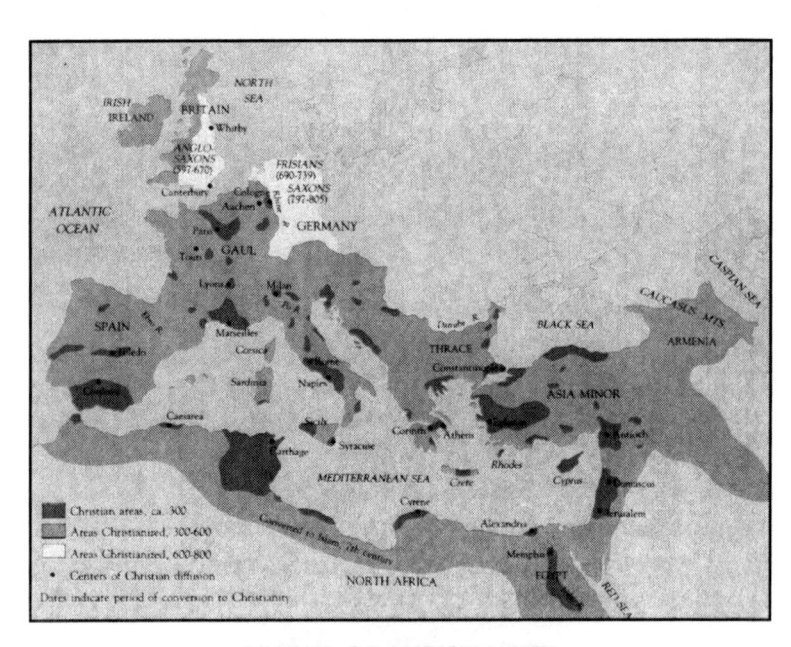

SPREAD OF CHRISTIANITY

(Courtesy of Wikipedia)

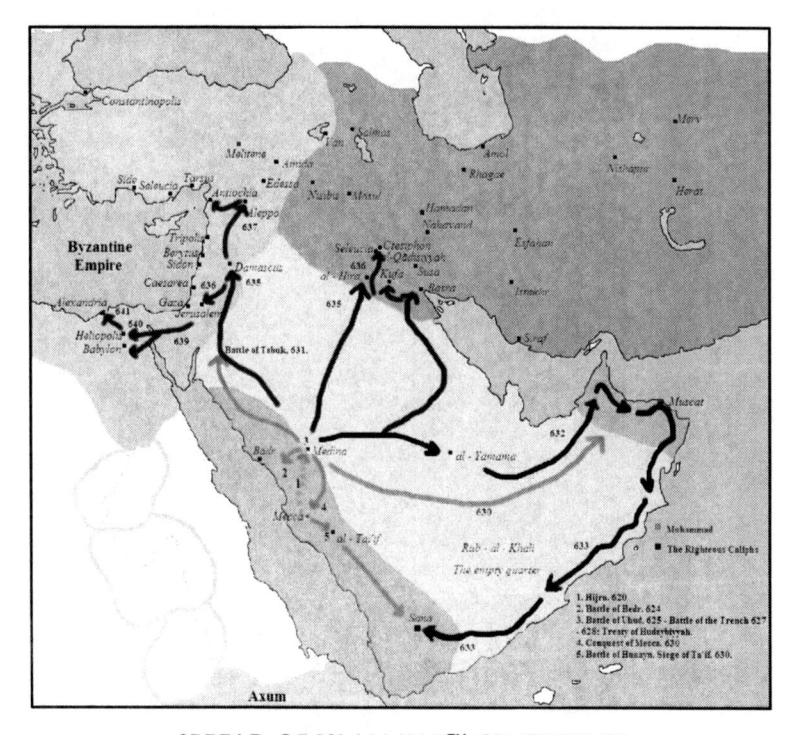

SPREAD OF ISLAM IN 7TH CENTURY CE
(Courtesy of Wikipedia)

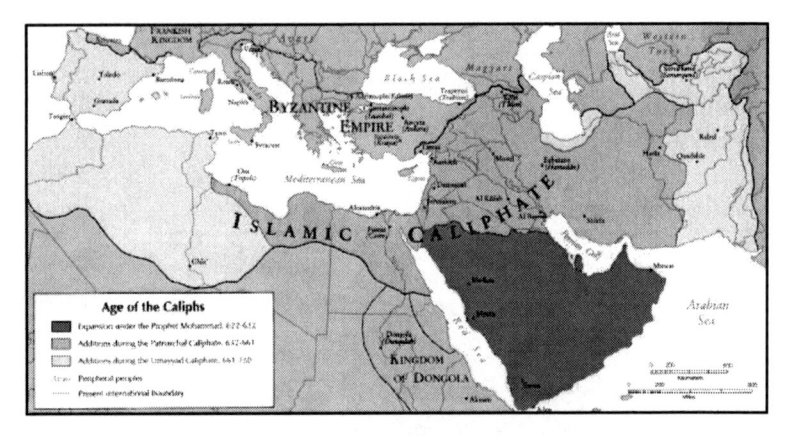

SPREAD OF ISLAM BY MID 8TH CENTURY CE
(Courtesy of Wikipedia)

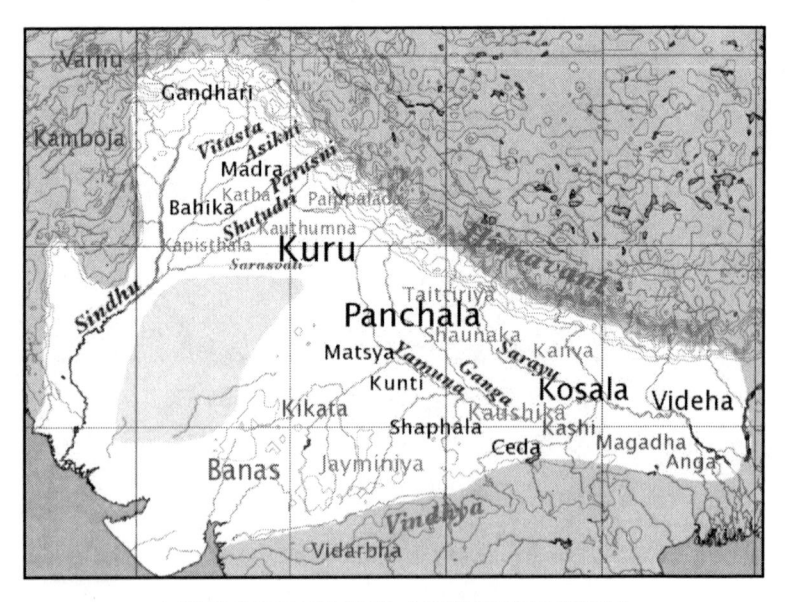

LATE VEDIC PERIOD, NORTHERN INDIA
(Courtesy of Wikipedia)

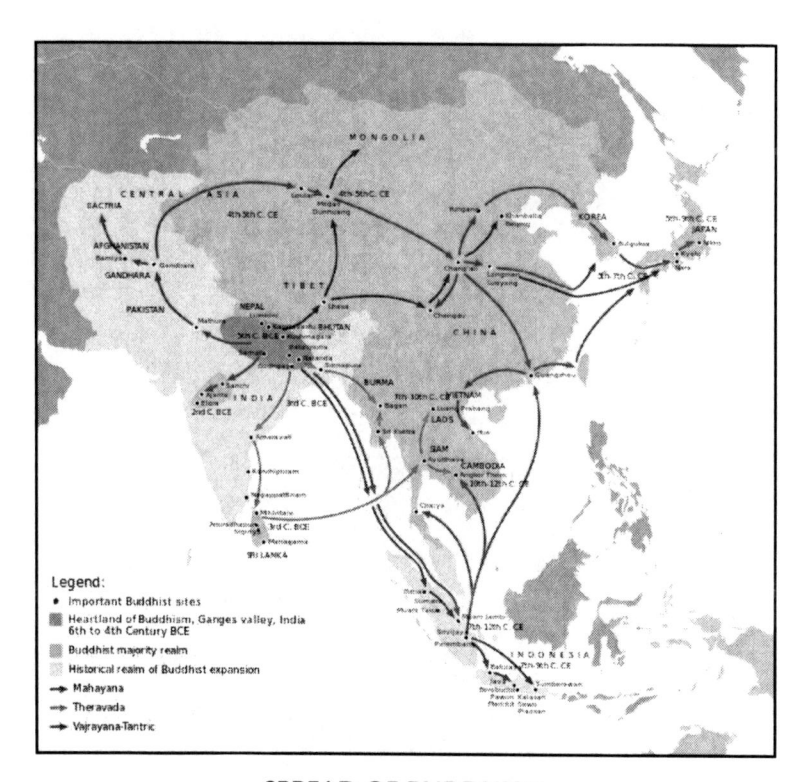

SPREAD OF BUDDHISM

(Courtesy of Wikipedia)

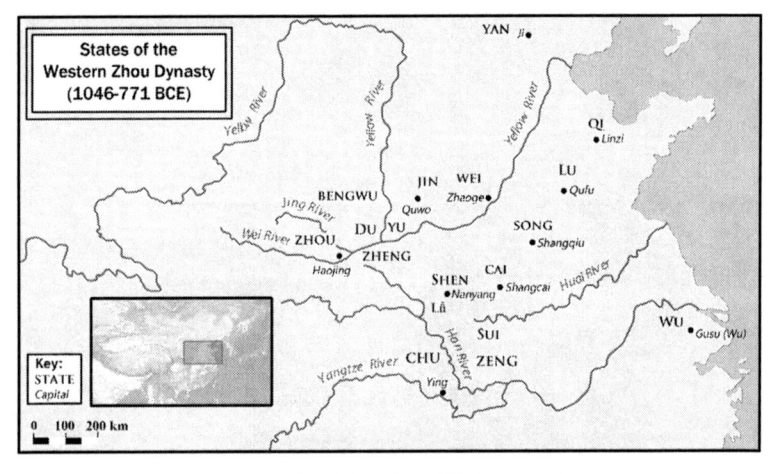

ZHOU DYNASTY

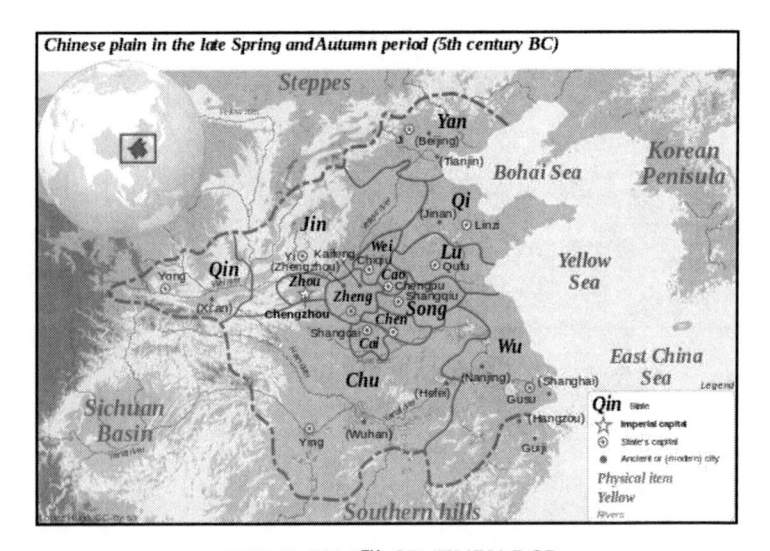

(Courtesy of Wikipedia)

CHINA BY 5TH CENTURY BCE

(Courtesy of Wikipedia)

Preface

Why? It is such a simple question. Children ask why from a very early age as they begin to learn basic concepts about their surroundings. They also ask what, how, where and who in their constant quest for discovery. These same questions mankind has pondered since our earliest ancestors roamed the planet. Humans have the ability to reason, which scientists believe separates us from other animals. It is this ability that has led our species from cave dwelling hunter-gatherers to the internet age and space exploration. We, like our children, are in search of answers. Children find their answers from parents and peers, as most of their questions can be answered based on simplicity. As we mature we realize some answers are not available to us. Sometimes they have yet to be uncovered, or may, in fact, be unattainable at the time. Scientists, theologians, explorers, and the like seek these truths in their own unique ways. So many questions remain unanswered in so many different arenas.

One underlying question however has mystified our

species since the aforementioned cave dwellers; why are we here, who put us here and what happens next? These questions coalesced with human thought resulting in the formation of religious beliefs. Just as our brains cannot fathom infinity, we likewise are unable to comprehend creation without a creator. We are born, thus have parental origins. How can the world we live in not have similar origins? It must have a creator or creators in our minds. Early man certainly would have pondered these same questions. Humanity could not have simply appeared out of thin air.

Early man tied creation to primitive deities and paid homage in an effort to improve their hunting success, fertility fortunes or their agricultural yields. As we evolved into more complex societal webs, religious worship subsequently evolved into more dynamic forms. A single religious belief that once permeated a clan was now the belief of an entire region. Settlements became cities, and territorial commonality became nations. A tribal elder who may have once led a sacrificial ritual to appease the god of the hunt was now a pharaoh, a caesar or an emperor governing a nation of believers worshiping the same god or gods. Religion slowly, yet methodically morphed from worship for the sole benefit of life on earth to happiness and success in whatever afterlife you believed to exist.

Mankind has suffered greatly as a result of religious affinity. Nearly all of our conflicts seem to be tied to differences in beliefs, often times religion is found at the core. Politics, warfare, money, persecution and other prejudices revolve around this dynamic. This brings us full circle to questions associated with our initial query. Why are we here? Who put us here?

What is our purpose? Where are we headed in life and in the afterlife if there is one? What else do we not know about the unknown?

This book is written attempting not to answer these long-sought puzzles, but to more clearly define the questions themselves. Mankind has become so confused in our quest that we have lost the sheer simplicity our infant brains asked in childhood. Perhaps by reflecting on our past and posing simple comparisons on our differences we can find some collective answers.

Origins

"Rivers, ponds, lakes and streams...they all have different names, but they all contain water. Just as religions do....they all contain truths"
Muhammad Ali

To the best of our knowledge it all began approximately 13.5 billion years ago. Theories suggest it originated as an infinitely hot and dense point of matter that in an instant exploded out with a bang. A rapid expansion followed at a speed incomprehensible to the human mind. After approximately one million years, star formation began taking place in interstellar nurseries. Soon galaxies formed and the young universe began to take shape. The stars and galaxies that were created in those early years were our sun's ancestors. The universe continued to expand outward over the billions of years that followed and star formation continued. Nearly 9 billion years after the Big Bang, in one of the spiral arms of a spiral galaxy we know today as the Milky Way, our solar system formed.

Planet Earth was created at this time as a rocky molten mass that eventually coalesced into a spherical world that settled into an orbit around the sun. Earth has been an inhospitable place for life forms for much of its history, and only in the last 500 million years has life flourished.

Fast forward the terrestrial clock to 2 million years ago and our story begins in Africa. Bipedal primates had evolved from their ape relatives a few million years earlier and inhabited portions of the continent. These hominids lived a nomadic existence as hunter-gatherers and thrived for hundreds of thousands of years in Africa. Eventually, growing populations or climate change forced some of these people to leave Africa for better hunting and foraging lands. *Homo erectus* was the first to migrate into other parts of the world about 1 million years ago. In the meantime other types of hominids developed and would follow *Homo erectus'* migration, *Homo sapiens* turn came about 70,000 years ago. Life would have been extremely difficult for these primitive humans. Infant mortality was staggeringly high, and for those who would survive childhood, disease, hunger and predation from wild animals were constant reminders of the frailties of life. Hunting and foraging were the jobs of each and every one in a group or clan. They likely had little time for anything else. Still, like modern humans, these early people would have certainly needed an escape. Mourning the death of a loved one would be a time for remorse. Conversely, childbirth, a new animal kill or victory in battle would have been cause for celebration, a release from the monotony of daily life. Celebration, or put more simply "play," was where it all started. As Robert Bellah points out in his book *Religion in Human Evolution*, play begins in children who are practicing for adulthood.[1] Playful interactions amongst early humans eventually led to rituals in these early times.[2]

Ritualistic behavior is a key component for the development of religion. The late anthropologist Clifford Geertz asserted that rituals create imaginary worlds.[3] Thus, imagination was vital in early religious thought. How do we define religion though? Is it easily explained? Is it possible to define religion? Like the emotion of love, it seems difficult to pinpoint a clear explanation. Merriam-Webster defines it in the following ways:

1. The service or worship of God or the supernatural; commitment or devotion to a religious faith or observance
2. A personal set or institutionalized system of religious attitudes, beliefs and practices
3. A cause, principle, or system of beliefs held to with ardor and faith

Another interesting and more complex definition comes from Bellah where he paraphrases Geertz:

Religion is a system of symbols that, when enacted by human beings, establishes powerful, pervasive, and long-lasting moods and motivations that make sense in terms of an idea of a general order of existence.[4]

---
1   Bellah, Robert. *Religion in Human Evolution*. Cambridge: Harvard University Press, 2011. Print. Pg. 91
2   Ibid
3   Bellah, preface xvi
4   Bellah, preface xiv

Geertz notably omits a reference to supernatural beings or gods. It seems he is arguing that religion has evolved by humans for humans to explain our existence in time and space. The late Emile Durkheim, who was a French sociologist added:

Religion is a system of beliefs and practices relative to the sacred that unite those who adhere to them in a moral community[5]

The varying definitions above certainly have commonality, but are clearly open to one's own interpretations. What we can comfortably conclude, however, is religious beliefs evolved from early stages as a relatively simple dynamic into the variety of beliefs we find in today's world.

Canadian neuroscientist and psychologist Merlin Donald believes religion has evolved over time in three stages: *Mimetic, mythic* and *theoretic*.[6] Mimetic belief systems may have begun as far back as 2 million years ago with *Homo erectus*. These early hominids would have mimicked one another in dance and ritual, and despite very limited oral communication skills, were able to convey beliefs and traditions to their peers. Music has long been able to speak to the soul of man and would have been a key ingredient in these early rituals. Music was a fundamental ingredient in the development of not only religion, but societies as a whole.[7] Bellah points to a tribe in central Brazil, *The Kalapalo*, as an example of its importance. To these people, virtually untouched from the outside world, music is the

---

5   Bellah, 1
6   Bellah, xviii
7   Ibid

language of the gods.[8] For them, the "powerful beings" speak music, people have their spoken languages, animals have distinctive calls, and inanimate things make noises.[9] No doubt, they are not historically alone in their devotion to the musical arts. Music, dance and ritual remained central in early beliefs for millennia. Not until the development of spoken language in the last 250,000 years did the mythical aspect of religious development transform early religion.[10]

Myths began as an integral part of religious stories accompanying the earlier ingrained rituals. Donald defines myth in the following way:

> *Mythical thought, in our terms, might be regarded as a unified, collectively held system of explanatory and regulatory metaphors. The mind has expanded its reach beyond the episodic perception of events, beyond the mimetic reconstruction episodes, to a comprehensive modeling of the entire human universe. Causal explanation, prediction, control......myth constitutes an attempt at all three; every aspect of life is permeated by myth.[11]*

Referring back to Merriam-Webster for the definition of myth we find:

1. A usually traditional story of ostensibly historical events that serves to unfold part of the world view

---
8   Bellah, 139
9   Ibid
10   Ibid
11   Bellah, 134-135

of a people or explain a practice, belief or natural phenomenon
2. A person or thing having only an imaginary or unverifiable existence

Stories passed down through generations and eventually led to theoretical analysis by scholars of the day. As *Homo sapiens* evolved from hunter-gatherer groups into a more complex, urban existence, it is likely theologians reorganized earlier rituals and beliefs to correspond to localized knowledge of the world. Armed with pragmatic beliefs and new ideas, religious ideology morphed from a primitive existence into an array of dogmas that would eventually circumnavigate the globe. No wonder it is nearly impossible to define religion or to quantify our belief systems!

Here Bellah paraphrases another Austrian sociologist Alfred Schutz:

> *"In spite of its apparent actuality, the world of daily life is a culturally, symbolically constructed world, not the world as it actually is. As such it varies in terms of time and space, with much in common across the historical and cultural landscape, but with occasional sharp differences."*[12]

Furthermore, Schutz argues we exist in our current space and time and work and live in this practical existence; life is based on a fundamental anxiety of (although not consciously), a fear of death.[13]

---

12   Bellah, preface xv
13   Bellah, 2

There is no question human beings have an anxiety of death, a fear we share with most other animals. What differentiates us is a cognitive recognition of the significance of death and a hope for an afterlife. The fact is we do not want to believe it all ends in death. It petrifies us and diminishes our innate belief of human importance; we are supposed to be different. Bellah notes an article published by evolutionary anthropologist Terrence Deacon, along with Tyrone Cashman, that describes three ways in which human abilities differentiate themselves from other primates.[14] The first is our ability to create narratives or stories. Our ape cousins have what is called episodic memory, which allows them to remember particular events and react accordingly when in a similar event.[15] Human beings, however, have the capacity to interrelate multiple events, creating narrative. The second difference is human beliefs of a dualistic nature of the visible world and the non-visible world.[16] Look no further than Pharaonic Egypt as an example. Egyptians believed the afterlife was an extension of humanity on earth. The pyramids and tombs they built were a portal to the afterlife, replete with all of their earthly needs, such as water, food and wealth. For the ancient Egyptians, the visible and non-visible worlds were intimately connected. Finally, Deacon and Cashman assert that humans seem to have a more advanced emotional capacity than other mammals.[17] All three of these elements of human psyche played an integral part in the development of, and nurturing of religious beliefs over time.

---

14 Bellah, 101
15 Ibid
16 Bellah, 102
17 Bellah, 103

As time passed, settlements grew, and soon formed alliances with other neighboring communities for stability and defense. Civilizations arose from these beginnings, and with them the citizenry commingled their varying ideals, including religious beliefs. Advances in technology, such as the advent of the wheel, cart, and plow allowed cultures such as those found in Egypt and Mesopotamia to flourish. Cities emerged by 3200 B.C.E., replete with temples and altars to worship and honor the gods. Writing developed in the same period, and scholars began systematically documenting current events. Written communication became the single most influential event in the history of religion. It transformed verbal ideology into tangible evidence for potential followers to witness and comprehend....in other words, religious ideas became credible.

As societies developed and evolved, religion grew more complicated. A strong religious base was vital in maintaining order in the new urban societies of the day. Kings were given divine mandate to rule from ancient Mesopotamia to China, often times claiming divinity in the flesh. Religious decrees assisted rulers in maintaining civility in an unforgiving world. After all, civil upheaval was more likely to develop in a godless society; fear of heavenly wrath helped to kept the peace. Across the globe, parallel dynamics were gripping ancient societies, and religious devotion was at the center. We begin in the Fertile Crescent....

Judaism

"The Lord said to Abram (Abraham): Go forth from the land of your kinsfolk and from your father's house to a land that I will show you. I will make of you a great nation, and I will bless you; I will make your name great, so that you will be a blessing. I will bless those who bless you and curse those who curse you. All the communities of the earth shall find blessing in you."

Genesis 12, 1-3

Early in the 2nd Millennium B.C.E., according to Jewish teachings in the book of *Genesis* in the *Tanakh* (Christian Bible's Old Testament), God appeared to a man named Abram to convince him to move his family away from the city/state of Ur. Ur located in the Fertile Crescent, was apparently in political decline, and it may have made sense for Abraham to comply with God's decree. His destination would be the Levant, one of the key routes out of Africa for our pre-historic ancestors.

This narrow region north of the Sinai Peninsula, described by University College London's Institute of Archaeology as the "crossroads of western Asia, the eastern Mediterranean, and northeast Africa," was the natural route of traveling parties spreading out to lands beyond Africa. A section of the Levant, now Israel and Palestine, borders the Syrian Desert to the east and the Mediterranean Sea to the west. This section became known in Biblical times as Canaan, the "Promised Land" by God to the Israelites, the descendants of Abraham. According to Jewish tradition, the descendants of Abraham lived in the Promised Land for many years before being enslaved in Egypt. After nearly four centuries of Egyptian servitude, the great prophet Moses, inspired by God and wielding divine powers, confronted the Egyptian Pharaoh demanding the release of the Israelites. After the Pharaoh refuted Moses ten times, Moses, with God's power, unleashed ten different plagues on Egypt after which Pharaoh finally relented. As the story is told in Exodus, Moses led the Israelites out of Egypt, ushering them back to their homeland. As the tribe left Egypt, Pharaoh changed his mind and decided to chase them down in order to slaughter them. The Egyptian Army caught up with the fleeing Israelites at the Red Sea. Before the onslaught could begin, Moses, again with divine intervention, parted the Red Sea to allow the Israelites to safely cross. Then the waters returned to drown the Egyptians in pursuit. God's chosen people were then free to continue their journey to the land God had promised them.

Most of us know the aforementioned story from our earliest days of religious study, Sunday school, catechism, and the like. It is a terrific narrative that is much more involved than this brief summary, and many scholars now believe it to be a story, a tall tale of biblical proportions, no pun intended.[18] . Some historians credit the first five books of the *Tanakh*, also known as the *Pentateuch or Torah*, as possibly having elements of truth embedded within its text, but believe as a whole it is more of a myth or a legend created by early Hebrew scholars. But why would they possibly make this up? What circumstances would prompt a group of individuals to create a story and lead people to believe it was actually factual? It all starts with the circumstances surrounding the people of Israel at the time the early books of the Old Testament were written. Abraham (if he actually existed) was believed to have lived sometime between the 17th-19th centuries B.C.E., and Moses apparently fled Egypt approximately 500 years later. The Pentateuch is believed to have been written 1000 years later, but no earlier than the 8th century B.C.E. and much of it may have been penned during the *Hellenistic Period*,[19]* Thus modern scholars credit much of the early Old Testament texts as having been developed to satisfy the need for historical significance of the people of Israel.[20] Archaeologists and sociologists today credit the beginning of the history of Judaism to the biblical story that began with Judges.[21] It is here we begin to look at the history and meaning of the Israelites.

The first recorded text of the existence of the Israelites was discovered by Victorian archaeologists in the 19th Century AD on a stone victory monument for the Egyptian Pharaoh

---

18 MacCulloch, Diarmaid. *Christianity: The First Three Thousand Years*. London: Viking, 2010. Print. pgs. 51-53
19 Bellah, 284
20 Smith, Houston. *The World's Religions*, New York: Harper Collins, 1991. Print. Pg. 272
21 MacCulloch, 52

Merneptah dated to the late 13th Century B.C.E. [22] The hieroglyphs on the monument indicated the Israelites were a collection of scattered peoples in the countryside as opposed to an organized civilization. According to Diarmaid MacCulloch in *Christianity, The First Three Thousand Years*, multiple accounts of Israelites, or "Hebrews" were found in early texts referring to them as *Habiru*, a social grouping living on the fringe of society. The *Habiru* would have been viewed as lower class farmers of little to no value in the eyes of the urban citizenry of larger kingdoms and empires. These farmers in the hills of Canaan were loosely organized in a scattered band of clans, much like what is found in the mountains of Afghanistan today. And, much like these modern Islamic clans that join forces to fight against "infidels," the hill peoples of Canaan aligned themselves in unity against foreign invaders of the day such as the Ammonites or the Philistines. According to scripture, there were twelve main clans or tribes in Israeli antiquity that were descended from the sons of Abraham's grandson, Jacob. In the latter centuries of the 2nd Millennia B.C.E. the entire Near East experienced an ancient dark age with Egyptian and Hittite Kingdoms in decline and the Assyrian Empire experiencing a series of setbacks. At the same time Israelite tribal leaders, or "judges" as they were referred to in the *Tanakh*, took advantage of the regional power vacuum resulting in the larger kingdoms' problems and the tribes built a stronger alliance. Ultimately, one judge/chieftain named Saul, became leader of a band of central hill clans and was pronounced the first "king" of Israel. According to Robert N. Bellah in *Religion in Human Evolution*, Saul was

---

22   MacCulloch, 53

only modestly more powerful than the judges who preceded him and did not have an army or a system of taxation.[23] Saul's reign was short-lived and he was subsequently overthrown by an upstart named David. David, known in infamy for slaying the Philistine giant named Goliath with a slingshot, went on to solidify complete control of Israel, organizing an army and capturing Jerusalem, making it the capital. He had a relatively lengthy reign and was succeeded by his son Solomon at his death. Solomon followed his father's success and the Kingdom of Israel reached its greatest extent under his reign. King Solomon erected a great temple in his time that purportedly housed the Arc of the Covenant, the golden chest said to have contained the Ten Commandments given to Moses centuries before. His reign lasted for approximately forty years and it was to be the last of a united Israel. Despite all of the success Israel realized during its unity, it was still a loosely organized coalition of tribes at its foundation and following Solomon's death the union dissolved. The split resulted in the Kingdom of Israel to the north and the Kingdom of Judah to the South. The Israelites would never again be able to reunite the divided kingdoms and would enjoy very little independence moving forward in their history.

Despite division of the kingdom following Solomon's death, the common bond of the Israelites was not in their geopolitical existence but in their religious and spiritual core. After all, they had heard the stories of the Exodus and their having been chosen as God's people. Unlike other Gods of the era, the

---

23   Bellah, 293

* term coined by 19th century A.D. scholars for Greek influence, post-Alexander, to differentiate its period from the Classical Greek period.

God of the Israelites cared about his people and their welfare. Conversely, in other cultures as in Greek, Roman and Egyptian, mankind was believed to be an afterthought of their respective deities who were more concerned with in-fighting and adultery.[24] The God of Israel later became known to his people as *Yahweh*, and as he had allegedly instructed to Moses on Mount Sinai, he was to have no equal. Yahweh is said to have revealed himself to the Israelites by choice dating back to the time of Abraham. He had shown them his love time and time again and expected a reciprocal devotion and respect from the people. But who was Yahweh and from where had he emerged? We do know that Israel got its name from a single god or a group of ancestors named "el." The name "Isra-el" literally means "El rules,"[25] which leads one to believe that Yahweh came later in Jewish tradition. Nevertheless, In those early days, it was common practice for Israelite families to pay homage to the memories of deceased clan leaders referring to them by the generic term of "el". In addition, the predominant deity found in much of the Israelite territory was called *El*, an ancient Ugaritic God.[26] * "El" had a wife, Asherah (Athirat), and children, one of the offspring named Yahweh. As noted in Deuteronomy, a portion of this ancient tale survives in Chapter 32:

> *When the most high (El) allotted peoples for inheritance,*
> *When He divided up humanity,*

---

[24] Smith, 275
[25] Bellah, 287
[26] Bellah, 294
*Ugarit was a northern coastal community that would have had influenced Israelites in the late 2nd Millennia B.C.E.

*He fixed the boundaries for peoples,
According to the number of divine sons:
For Yahweh's portion is his people,
Jacob his own inheritance.*
(Deuteronomy 32: 8-9)

So Yahweh inherits the people of Jacob (Israel) in this account and other divine sons of El inherit people in other lands. So why has El not survived history as "The God" of the Israelites? Maybe the fact that the above passage indicates Yahweh's ownership of the Israelites gave them an affinity for his subsequent worship. Thus, if the Ugaritic hierarchy is accurate, could Yahweh have absorbed the worship of his father El over the course of time in Hebrew tradition? Psalm 89 is *A Lament over God's Promise to David*, and verse 26 is as follows:

*I will set his hand upon the sea,
His right hand upon the rivers.*

According to later scripture, the above passage is clearly intended to refer to Yahweh, yet ancient Ugaritic myths attribute El to conquering the chaos of the water, streams and rivers, while creating the world.[27] Absorption of worship has certainly been commonplace in the history of religious practices. Indoctrination of old ideals into new religious arenas has seen church leaders in many early faiths include elements of older practices to appease the minds of the converts and ease their transition into the new faith. Many elements remain and

---
27   Bellah, 292

build their own traditions in these new faiths. We see an example of this today in alters where "sacrifices" are being made in churches worldwide. They are sacramental and symbolic, yet send a clear reference to their ritualistic pagan origins.

Following the split of Israel, the southern kingdom of Judah retained Jerusalem as its capital and became somewhat of an isolationist state guarding their precious temple and its belongings. The northern kingdom, retaining the name Israel, was more cosmopolitan than their southern rivals with a major international trade route running through the Megiddo Pass located in their territory.[28] For the next two centuries each kingdom would struggle with establishing themselves as regional players in international affairs. This period saw the rise of the great Jewish prophets we find in scripture such as Elijah, Hosea, Micah and Isaiah to name a few. Many of the prophets concerned themselves with political positions of the day, while others focused on the religious aspect of the people. One notable characteristic many of the prophets shared was a devout following of the worship of Yahweh and the discouragement of worshipping any other gods in his place. The prophets, however, appear to have been in a small minority in the exclusive worship of Yahweh. There is widespread historical and archaeological evidence of polytheistic practices throughout Israel at that time at all levels of socio-economic classes.[29] So clearly, Yahweh had become a relatively central figure in Hebrew culture during this period, yet it would not be until later that he emerges as the central figure of Hebrew worship.

---

[28] MacCulloch, 56
[29] Bellah, 298-305

In the late 8th Century B.C.E., the Northern Kingdom of Israel was overrun by a resurrected Assyrian Empire and witnessed many of its citizens exiled. Some refugees fled to Judah where Jerusalem and outlying communities saw their populations swell considerably. About twenty years later Assyria and its ruler, Sennacherib, turned on Judah.[30] Accounts differ as to details, but what is clear is forty-six fortified settlements surrounding Jerusalem, many presumably containing former refugees from the north, were sacked and Sennacherib laid siege to Jerusalem. The town never fell, but Judah was made a vassal state and would pay tribute to Assyria for nearly a century to follow. Expectations of Judah certainly would have included sending material gifts to Assyria, accepting Sennacherib as the ultimate ruler, and the recognition of the Assyrian high god Assur. Failure to honor the agreement may have resulted in swift and ruthless punishment on the people of Judah. It is in this period Yahweh appears to become more central in Hebrew theology. The Israelites saw their vassal treaty with Assyria as a covenant they must uphold to prevent bad things from happening to their people. This was interpreted as a similar duty they had to their god, Yahweh.[31] They strongly believed their position as a servant to Assyria was all part of God's plan for them; Assyria was simply following Yahweh's course of action. It is no coincidence that the fifth and final book of the *Tanakh*, Deuteronomy, was supposedly found by the High Priest in the Temple of Jerusalem in 621 B.C.E.[32] This miraculous discovery may have been a ruse, however, as scholars had likely been secretly putting together this final

---

30 2 Kings 18:13
31 Bellah, 305-308
32 MacCulloch, 60

book of the Pentateuch for decades.[33] Deuteronomy was written to reinforce the importance of Yahweh's covenant with the Israelites dating back to the time of Abraham and reintroduced Moses as a great prophet and servant of Yahweh. It coincided with the decline of Assyrian power in the region and reinvigorated the Israelites in Judah with hope for a brighter future. Alas, that immediate effect was short-lived.

The fall of Assyria saw the rise of a new Babylonian Empire under *Nebuchadnezzar II*. Under his military command, Babylonian armies wiped out the Assyrians in their capital of Nineveh in 612 B.C.E. Babylon and Egypt would then begin a dual conquest over much of the territory located between the two empires. Judah was no exception to the conquest. Following a pro-Egyptian movement in Jerusalem, Nebuchadnezzar invaded the city. The initial invasion took place in 599 B.C.E. and in just three months Jerusalem fell to Babylonian forces.[34] The city was plundered and many prominent citizens were exiled to Babylon.[35] Nebuchadnezzar appointed a king, *Zedekia*h, to rule over the territory in his stead and returned to his homeland. In less than a decade Zedekiah betrayed Nebuchadnezzar and revolted against Babylon by forming another alliance with Egypt, prompting Nebuchadnezzar to once again return to Judah. This time he laid siege to the city for nearly two years, and by 586 B.C.E., Babylonian forces had destroyed Solomon's temple, plundered the city and enslaved many of the remaining citizens

---

33 Bellah, 308
34 2 Chronicles 36:9
35 2 Kings 24:14

to join those already exiled in Babylon.[36] He killed all his appointed king's sons before their father's eyes. As for Zedekiah himself, after witnessing his sons' deaths, the king had his eyes put out so his final sight was the slaying of his offspring. He was then taken away to Babylon as a prisoner until his death.[37] For the next half century many of the Israelites who were spared Babylonian exile relocated to the town of *Mizpah*[38], which served as the capital of the new Babylonian province of *Yehud Medinata* (literally meaning the "Province of Judah" in Aramaic). In 539 B.C.E., Cyrus the Great of Persia conquered Babylon and allowed any of the Jews living there the opportunity to return to their homeland.[39] Although some stayed in Babylon, content under Cyrus' reign, many chose to return to Israelite territories. Cyrus, and later Persian rulers, helped citizens of Jerusalem rebuild their holy temple, and by 516 B.C.E. it was restored on the original site of its predecessor. Surprisingly enough, help offered by the people of Judah who had not been exiled was refused. It is evident that considerable animosity existed between the post-exilic Jews and the ones whom had remained. Maybe it was a resentment by the former for their brethren not sharing in the anguish of Babylonian exile, or perhaps a societal snub being that the exiled were the Jewish elite and those left behind were of little political or religious importance. Nevertheless, a prejudice remained for centuries to follow. The time in Babylon did much to change the psyche of the Hebrew people. They absorbed new ideas from their captors, most notably influences from

---

36   Jeremiah 52: 13-30
37   Jeremiah 52: 10-11
38   Jeremiah 40: 6-12
39   Ezra 1:1-4, 2 Chronicles 36:22-23

the Babylonian religion of *Zoroastrianism*. Zoroastrians believe in a supreme being, *Ahura Mazda*, an evil agent *Angra Mainyu*, and a savior who will absolve banished souls of their sins and reunite them with their maker at the end of time. The aforementioned beliefs are central in many religions today and clearly had an effect on Jewish interpretations at the time. What really puzzled the post-exilic Israelites was how could Yahweh have brought more anguish upon the people of Israel? Could they have broken the covenant again, a pact the Deuteronomic Revolution warned against? Maybe there was another party involved to disrupt things and interfere with God's plans? Thus, an idea of an "adversary" or "opposer" to God appeared at this time that was powerful enough to intervene. He was referred to as *Hassatan*, or Satan.[40] It made perfect sense after the influences Zoroastrianism had on the Hebrew psyche. Angra Mainyu and Satan were likely, in their eyes, the same evil master whose sole purpose was to thwart Yahweh's plans for the Israelites.

    Persia would control Judea for nearly two centuries before the region was overrun in the late 4th century B.C.E. by the great Macedonian forces led by Alexander the Great. Alexander died shortly after gaining control of much of his vast empire, and after his death the territories were divided up amongst his top generals. The Levant was initially controlled by one of Alexander's top generals, Ptolemy, who ruled Egypt beginning in 323 B.C.E. following Alexander's death. Ptolemy's empire would control the territory for more than a century to follow. The Ptolemaic Empire would battle the Seleucid Empire over control of Israelite territory for much of

---

[40] MacCulloch, 63

the period, and by 198 B.C.E. the Seleucids would finally gain control for good. The Seleucid Empire, just as the Ptolemaic Empire, was ruled by descendants of the Macedonians under Alexander. All of these empires were collectively referred to as *Hellenistic*, a term coined by 19th century A.D. scholars for Greek influence, post-Alexander, to differentiate its period from the Classical Greek period. Thirty years later, Seleucid King *Antiochos IV* attacked Jerusalem to suppress a revolt as chronicled below:

> *"When these happenings were reported to the king, he thought that Judea was in revolt. Raging like a wild animal, he set out from Egypt and took Jerusalem by storm. He ordered his soldiers to cut down without mercy those whom they met and to slay those who took refuge in their houses. There was a massacre of young and old, a killing of women and children, a slaughter of virgins and infants. In the space of three days, eighty thousand were lost, forty thousand meeting a violent death, and the same number being sold into slavery."*
> **2 Maccabees 5: 11-14**

Shortly after the slaughter, the king issued a decree outlawing Jews from following the customs of their religion, ordered a desecration of the temple and instructed the citizens to take the Greek god Zeus as their own.[41] Coupled with the previous slaughter, this was too much to handle for the Israelites. A civil war/rebellion ensued beginning in 166 B.C.E., led by Judas

---
41 2 Maccabees 6: 1-12

Maccabeus, and after years of terrible bloodshed, Hellenistic rule in Judea came to an end. Two decades later, after numerous power struggles for the region, Judas' brother, Simon, gained control of Israel and established the first independent Jewish state since Solomon. The new Israelite nation became known as the *Hasmonean Dynasty* and ruled Judea for much of the next century before succumbing to Roman expansion in 63 B.C.E. It would be two millennia before Israel would be made whole again.

Deportations, exiles, commerce and travel had spread the Jewish people since the days of David and Solomon. The opportunity to worship at the temple in Jerusalem was not afforded people living far away, and communities developed their own religious centers in lieu of the temple. Synagogues, as they became known, became the spiritual centers of the Hebrew faith. Greek influence remained embedded in the Judean culture for some time, and little changed after Rome controlled the area as the Romans, too, had been strongly influenced by their Greek counterparts. According to MacCulloch, in *2 Maccabees*, the suggestion that God created the world out of nothing was a new concept in Jewish writings, a definitive Greek ideal.[42] This ideal coincided with a new idea of an afterlife. There was very little mention of an afterlife in much of the Old Testament, and all indications were that all life ceased to exist at death.[43] In addition, a prevailing belief held that the Maccabean Rebels, who gave their lives so bravely, should be rewarded in some form or fashion. Here, Greek influence is once again evidenced in Plato's *The Republic*. It

---

42   MacCulloch, 70
43   Ibid

documents *The Myth of Er*, which describes a tale of warriors killed in battle, who are posthumously resurrected in their spirit to an afterlife, and further describes the banishment of the immoral human beings to a netherworld. The banishment to a netherworld would certainly have coincided in Jewish minds with the Greek belief of an underworld for deceased souls named *Tartarus* governed by the god *Hades*. At some point the story of Hades being God's adversary, merged with the concept of Satan. The belief of an afterlife was controversial at the time, but the new Jewish sect, later to become known as Christians, took the belief and ran with it.

Christianity

For God so loved the world that he gave his only Son, so that everyone who believes in him might not perish but might have eternal life. For God did not send his Son into the world to condemn the world, but that the world may be saved through him.

John 3, 16-17

In the middle of the 8th Century B.C.E. as the Assyrians were conquering the Northern Kingdom of Israel, far to the west, on the other side of the Mediterranean Sea, a city was founded. According to legend from Livy's *History of Rome*, in the year 753, twin brothers named Romulus and Remus established the city of Rome on the banks of the Tiber River. Located on a section of river that was easily forded, it was an ideal spot for a city, as travel and commerce flourished along the river's course. Local clans populated Rome in its early history, and over time tribes from surrounding hills and valleys joined the community.[44] Romulus had been the first king of Rome, and a monarch continued to be the head of government for over two centuries. As the years passed, the city grew from a small riverside trading center to a regional power controlling a good portion of central Italy. In approximately 509 B.C.E. the monarchy was overthrown and a republic established. For the next half millennia, the Roman Republic would be governed by the people. Slowly, the republic expanded its sphere of influence, and within two centuries, controlled virtually the entire Italian Peninsula. Still, Rome remained a far cry from being a major player on the international stage. Greece, under command of Alexander the Great and his successors was the world's greatest empire of the day. In addition, on the northern coast of Africa, the Phoenician port city of Carthage had become a dominant force in Mediterranean affairs. In the year 264, Roman armies fought on foreign soil for the first time in the first of three wars against Carthage. Known as the Punic Wars, the three successive conflicts spanned over a century. While not at war with Carthage, Rome engaged the Hellenistic Kingdoms which had been divided up amongst Alexander's generals at his death. By the middle of the 2nd Century B.C.E. Rome had conquered them all, as well as Carthage, and controlled much of the known world. A century later, Julius Caesar, on the verge of potentially reclaiming the Roman monarchy, was assassinated by his colleagues in the Roman Senate. A power struggle erupted following the famous assassination, and *Gaius Octavius (Octavian)*, Julius' great-nephew and adopted heir, emerged victorious. He soon

---

44   Goldsworthy, Adrian. *Caesar: Life of a Colossus*. New Haven: Yale University Press, 2006. Print. pg. 14

became the first emperor of the Roman Empire, taking the name Caesar Augustus; the Roman Empire was officially established.

Meanwhile, back across the Mediterranean, the *Hasmonean Dynasty* of Judea came to an end, and *Herod the Great*, a Roman loyalist, assumed control of the vassal state. Roman influence had been prominent in the region for over two decades when Herod was pronounced ruler in 37 B.C.E. Hasmonean rule had given Jews a brief respite from foreign dominion, but Roman subjugation was a cruel reminder of Israel's political history. To fund the massive Roman budget, Judeans were crippled with a massive tax burden.[45] Most citizens could scarcely make ends meet, and only the *Sadducees* (Jewish upper class) were able to afford the status quo.[46] The Israelites longed for a return of the glory days of David and Solomon. Whispers of salvation began to resonate amongst the Hebrew people. Long had they yearned for deliverance by Yahweh, yet despite hopes and prayers, they were constantly being conquered and subjugated. Ancient prophecies dating back to the writings of the post-exilic Jews in the 6th Century B.C.E. spoke of a "messiah" or "savior" who would come to rule Israel and bring a new order of existence to the world. Prophetic excerpts are found scattered throughout the Old Testament:

> *"For a child is born to us, a son is given us; upon his shoulder dominion rests. They name him Wonder-Counselor, God-Hero, Father-Forever, Prince of Peace.*

---

[45] Smith, 321
[46] Ibid

His dominion is vast and forever peaceful, From David's throne, and over his kingdom, which he confirms and sustains By judgment and justice, both now and forever. The zeal of the Lord of hosts will do this!"
=Isaiah 9, 5-6

"But he was pierced for our offenses, crushed for our sins, Upon him was the chastisement that makes us whole, by his stripes we were healed. We had all gone astray like sheep, each following his own way; But the Lord laid upon him the guilt of us all"
=Isaiah 53: 5-6

"But you, Bethlehem-Ephrathah too small to be among the clans of Judah, From you shall come forth for me one who is to be ruler in Israel; Whose origin is from of old, from ancient times. Therefore the Lord will give them up, until the time when she who is to give birth has borne, and the rest of his brethren shall return to the children of Israel. He shall stand firm and shepherd his flock by the strength of the Lord, his God; And they shall remain, for now his greatness shall reach to the ends of the earth; he shall be peace."
=Micah 5: 1-4

So as the people of Judea watched the Roman legions march through their land, in their hearts and minds were the hopes of ancient prophecies being fulfilled. When was this savior coming and what type of salvation would he bring them? Will salvation be in this life or in a life to come?

CHRISTIANITY | 27

Regardless, for the children of Israel, all they had, as always, was hope.

Herod is known to have died in the year 4 B.C.E., and most modern scholars believe, shortly before his death, Jesus of Nazareth was brought into the world.[47] Little is known about the early life of Jesus Christ. Only two of the four Gospels in the New Testament mention his childhood, and they have differing accounts. This has led some scholars to question the accuracy of the nativity narrative, so we will move ahead to his adult life, beginning in the 2nd decade of the 1st Century C.E.[48]

Jesus was raised in the Jewish faith one thousand years after the glory days of David's Kingdom. According to scripture, he emerged as a public figure around the age of thirty. Accompanied by twelve disciples he had selected to assist in his mission, he began preaching to the people of Judea new ideas in the Jewish faith. At the time, four factions existed among the Jewish people. The aforementioned *Sadducees* comprised one sect, one which was content with their situation as a vassal to Rome. The *Pharisees*, seeking divine intervention from Yahweh, looked to strictly adhere to the ancient laws written in the Old Testament in hopes of securing God's favor. The Essenes and Zealots were extremists, the former choosing to shrink away from the world and live a life of piety, and the latter were militants looking for armed intervention with Rome. Jesus offered another option, one of compassion and love. The Jewish people had become overly engrossed with rules and regulations in Jesus' day. They were

---

[47] Ibid, 318, Diarmaid MacCulloch, *Christianity, The First Three Thousand Years*, 82
[48] Vermes, Geza. *The Nativity: History and Legend*. London: Penguin Books, 2006. Print

expected to live a life of purity and sanctity that rivaled the perceived perfection and holiness of Yahweh. These expectations lead to social and religious divisions among the Jews. The lower class people were ostracized by the more "worthy" individuals comprising the religious elite. Jesus held to a belief that this approach by his faith was a misrepresentation of how God judged his people; in contrast, God is compassionate for all individuals pure in spirit. Stories abound in the New Testament of Jesus blessing prostitutes, tax collectors, and other social outcasts of the day who may have had an unpopular, even dirty profession, yet were filled with love. Conversely, many of the self-righteous priests and upper class citizens were chastised by Jesus for not living a life of love and compassion. That is what made him so polarizing for those who were alive to witness his benevolence in the short time he evangelized in the hills of Judea. Christianity was to be a religion of equals; love one another as you do yourselves, and love even your enemies Jesus preached. He gave the common people hope at a time when they had every reason to be extremely pessimistic about their existence. He was known to perform miracles healing the sick, reversing disease and recalling life from the dead. He proclaimed himself to be the Messiah, the Son of God prophesized in the Old Testament who was sent to save mankind. Unfortunately, he knew his fate had a terrible ending.

The Sadducees and Pharisees were threatened by Jesus' presence. The Sadducees liked their situation and did not wish for change. They lived very well, and despite having to pay tribute to Rome, were, for the most part, in control of Jerusalem. The Pharisees were simply baffled by Jesus' assertions about religion and viewed him a heretic. The two groups ultimately conspired to have the Roman authorities arrest Jesus and charge him with blasphemy and treason. Convicted, despite little evidence levied against him, Jesus was sentenced to death. Flogged, scorned, and adorned with a crown of thorns he was led through the streets of Jerusalem to the outer gates of the city. It is there that he was nailed to a wooden cross and raised up for display. The man, who many of his disciples thought would save them from Roman oppression, was about to die. He had incessantly warned them this was his destiny, yet none took him seriously. Within three days of his death, scripture says he was resurrected from the dead and walked the earth in an otherworldly form, occasionally appearing to his followers for a short period of time (forty days is commonly accepted) at which point he ascended into heaven. This was the final miracle, if you will, one which certainly convinced those who witnessed the event of his divinity.

The disciples of Jesus would dedicate the rest of their lives preaching the "Good News" their savior had shared with them to much of the known world. Other people joined the early evangelists, most notably a tent maker named Saul who actively persecuted Christians as a youth, only to convert to Christianity after Jesus appeared to him in a vision. From that point on Paul, as he was thus known, spent the rest of his life sowing the seeds of the young church. Paul would be martyred for his commitment to the new faith, along with nearly all of Christ's original disciples. In these formative years, Christianity remained a sect of Judaism. At first small groups met independent of the mainstream Jews in community synagogues. But then in 66 C.E., Jewish rebels (The Zealots) revolted against Roman occupation in Jerusalem and killed the Sadducee elite in the process. Over the next four years Jerusalem was under Jewish control, until Roman armies laid siege to the city. Jerusalem fell, and the great Temple was destroyed. Christians fled the city and established their unofficial headquarters in the northeastern town of Pella, and the Jews regrouped in the Mediterranean coastal town of Jamnia (Yavneh). The Christians wanted to distance themselves from the rebellious Jews, yet eventually the Jewish faith regained the favor of Rome. It may have helped the Christian case to remain connected to Judaism, which enjoyed religious freedom from Rome. Nevertheless, Christianity became autonomous of its parent religion and a target of the Empire. Imperial authority tolerated opposing faiths as long as they had a historical foundation, Judaism included.[49] Rome was a pagan empire that worshipped multiple gods, mirroring its Greek neighbors to the east. Yet, they respected other religions to a point. Thus, by separating from the Jews, Christianity was not in a favorable political position. Early Christians did not ally themselves with fellow citizens, either. They were a secretive group that kept their religious practices, as well as their daily lives, hidden. Non-participation in common Roman activities from festivals to bath houses further raised suspicion of the new sect.[50] By the latter half of the 3rd Century CE, Christians were being actively persecuted by Roman Imperial decree. The persecution culminated under the rule of Emperor Diocletian beginning in the year 303, which saw churches destroyed and mass

---

49 MacCulloch, 155-156
50 MacCulloch, 157-159

executions of Christians throughout the empire. In fact, nearly half the martyred in early Christianity met their fate during this period. Soon, however, the adage of "it must get worse before it gets better" was certainly applicable to Christian history. In less than a decade, Christianity went from being openly persecuted by the Emperor Diocletian, to the official church of the Roman Empire under Constantine the Great.

Having Imperial support, Christianity was free to grow. It expanded from a regional institution in the Eastern Mediterranean to outposts throughout the Roman Empire and beyond. At the same time, the Roman Empire had split into two independent governing bodies, the western seat remained in Rome, and the new city of Constantinople the governmental seat of the east. Yet despite unprecedented growth, the church was bitterly divisive in these early times. The crucifixion, resurrection, reappearance and ascension of Jesus confounded early religious scholars from the beginning. The fact the Gospels do not go into much detail about the resurrection and ascension made it all the more perplexing. But what the early church wrestled with the most was the incarnation of Jesus and the structure of the divine. Paul mentioned in his writings the "Spirit" that was so familiar to Jews of the day, with allusions back to the Book of Genesis. Later, in the then-Roman colony of Carthage, a well-educated man named Tertullian began writing about the church's growing pains.[51] Included in his manuscripts is the first documented usage of the term *Trinitas*, referring to the Holy Trinity of God, Jesus and the Holy Spirit.[52] The first Ecumenical council, the first

---

51 MacCulloch, 144-145
52 Ibid

church conclave, was ordered by Constantine to be held in Nicaea in the year 325. Nicaea was a convenient location for Constantine, whose headquarters was in the nearby town of Nicomedia. The key issue was two differing beliefs that Jesus and God were separate or united beings. Seems rather trivial in our time, but it was a heated debate for the early church. The council ultimately found that God and Jesus, or father and son, were one. Jesus, was "of one substance" with the father, or in other words "consubstantial with the father".[53] This became part of the *Nicene Creed*, which originated at the council, and is still echoed in many Christian churches to this day. Half a century later, the second ecumenical council met in Constantinople, and among the many things discussed was the equality of the Holy Spirit to Father and the Son.[54] An Eastern Church leader named Macedonius led a movement to make the Holy Spirit subordinate of God and Jesus.[55] The Council of Constantinople thought otherwise, and officially made the three members of the Holy Trinity equal.

By the fifth century, the church had four major seats (*sees*) of power located in Antioch, Rome, Alexandria and Constantinople.[56] Each Holy See had its own religious and political agendas and they were often times at odds with one another, most notably Alexandria and Antioch.[57] The majority of Christianity was still located in the Eastern Mediterranean realm. Coupled with the gradual decline of the Roman Empire, notably in the west, the Roman See was fighting to

---

[53] MacCulloch, 215-217
[54] MacCulloch, 219
[55] Ibid
[56] Jenkins, Philip. *Jesus Wars*. New York: Harper Collins, 2010, pgs. 78-79
[57] Jenkins, 80

remain relevant.[58] The foundation of Peter, Paul and the early church was the only selling point for Rome. Constantinople was considered the "new Rome," a splendid city Constantine the Great had built less than a century before, certainly the crown jewel of the Eastern Roman Empire.[59] Antioch and Alexandria were the two intellectual centers of the church. More importantly, each of these two possessed differing beliefs in the nature of Jesus Christ, one that would tear apart the Christian world forever.

In the year 428, Nestorius, a disciple of the church of Antioch, became the newly appointed archbishop of Constantinople. He wasted no time in making himself out to be a very controversial appointment, with aggressive, hardline agendas.[60] In November of the same year, Nestorius' chaplain, Anastasius, asserted in a sermon in Constantinople that Christians should not refer to the Virgin Mary as *Theotokos*, or God-Bearer, but more appropriately call her *Christokos*, or Mother of Christ.[61] This was in accordance with Nestorius' views that Jesus' divine and human natures formed a loose union.[62] This essentially minimalized the divinity of Christ, a heretical concept, especially for those from the Patriarchate of Alexandria who held the belief that Jesus was wholly divine.[63] This resulted in two decades of friction in Christendom. Not only was the church in a quandary, the Roman Empire was in serious danger of unraveling at the seams. Gaiseric, as leader of the Vandal Empire had captured Carthage and threatened

---

58 Jenkins, 89-90
59 Jenkins, 79-80
60 Jenkins, 132
61 Jenkins, 42
62 Jenkins, 134
63 Jenkins, 57-58

to invade Alexandria, and eventually Rome. At the same time, Attila and his Hun armies were threating to sack Gaul. The new Roman Emperor Marcian, ordered a new council to meet in autumn of 451 in the Constantinople suburb of Chalcedon. This group would not only decide the future of the church, but the future of the Roman Empire. On one side was Alexandria and the belief of Christ's "one nature," completely divine. They were known as the *Monophysites*.[64] The Nestorian followers continued to promote their belief systems at Chalcedon. Finally the followers of the Church of Antioch, the *Dyophysites*, believed he was divine in spirit yet was completely incarnate on earth; or wholly god and wholly man.[65] Ultimately, this dual nature of Christ that Antioch promoted was deemed the official position of the church at the conclusion of the council and remains so to this day. The Nestorians and The Monophysites rejected Chalcedon and ultimately broke from the church to form their own independent Christian Churches. As for the invading armies of Attila and Gaiseric, the Huns invaded Italy, but stopped short of Rome due to logistics. Rome was not as lucky with Gaiseric, however, as The Vandals sacked and plundered the city in 455.

The early Christian world was predominant to the east of the Italian Peninsula. Slowly however, with the aid of Islam's rise, its destiny lay to the west. Barbaric and uneducated, Western Europe gradually emerged from the shadows of ignorance. The Frankish King Clovis I converted to Christianity late in the 5th Century and demanded everyone under his dominion to follow suit. His Merovingian Dynasty ruled much

---

64   Jenkins, xi (introduction)
65   Ibid

of Western Europe for the next two and a half centuries. Missionary work soon spread throughout the continent. By the early 9th Century, largely due to Charlemagne's influence, scholastic devotion to Christian learning became paramount, and by the start of the 2nd millennium, nearly all of Europe was under Christian rule. Internal and external conflicts would define the next thousand years of Christianity. From military crusades to recapture lost lands, to bitter divisiveness over secular positions, battles raged.

Eventually Christianity fractured into many divisions. Martin Luther was certainly a huge catalyst in this divisiveness in the early 16th Century.[66] Yet, despite the turmoil, Christianity thrived. Europeans settled the Americas around this same time and brought their faith with them. Today it is the largest religion in the world. What made Christianity so enticing for people then, as it does today, is self-empowerment. As in many other faiths, burdens are lifted from the shoulders of a Christian upon belief in Jesus. Fear of death is the first, as Christ instilled in his followers an inner strength that would be able to overcome earthly perils, including death. Christians are released from their sense of guilt that builds up over the course of time in the human psyche. And finally, it relieves the human ego of its sense of selfishness by allowing someone to love others unconditionally, like Christ loves us. By dying on the cross, Jesus atoned for the sins of mankind. There is no power stronger in the world than love, and this is the basis of Christianity.

---

66   MacCulloch, 604

Islam

"La ilaha illa 'llah."
(There is no god but God, and Muhammad is His messenger.)

(Islam's Confession of Faith)

Rewinding the sands of time in the Middle East, a time traveler from today would find a much different place 1500 years ago. Decidedly Muslim in the 21st Century, the Middle East was the heart of the Christian World in the first few centuries after Jesus' death. Rome, a western outpost of the church, was the only of the five Holy Sees of Christianity located in Europe. Alexandria was located in northern Africa. Antioch, Jerusalem and Constantinople were in Asia. Modern Bagdad was built only a few miles from the ruins of the Sassanian (Persian) capital of Seleucia-Ctesiphon, an important early Christian center. Christian churches dotted the landscapes of modern day Afghanistan and Pakistan, even reaching into China and India. Still, Christianity was a fractured religion at the time.

The Orthodox Churches in Rome and Constantinople maintained their view on Jesus' divine nature, and the majority of Nestorian and Monophysite Christians sought religious asylum in Persian lands.[67] Initially, these Christians met severe persecution by Sassanian authorities, comparable to early Roman persecution, and thousands were slaughtered. The Sassanian state religion was the traditional Persian religion of Zoroastrianism, which was a fire cult, similar to early Vedic worship in India, but was also monotheistic and had many similarities to modern religions. Eventually, Persians became more tolerant of other religions and allowed Christian sects, rejected by the west, to flourish under their rule. Persia and Rome had been at each other's throats for centuries, and conflict between the two was virtually endless throughout the 6th Century CE. It culminated in 614, when Persian forces captured Jerusalem, slaughtered the clergy, men, women and children and desecrated churches and holy relics.

While the Roman and Persian Empires were tearing themselves apart, the forgotten Arabian Peninsula was a desert wasteland of polytheistic Bedouin tribes. Inter-tribal warfare and blood feuds were incessant. In addition, promiscuity and gambling permeated an immoral society teetering on collapse. By the end of the 6th Century, the most important city in Arabia both economically and spiritually was Mecca. Located along an important trade route, traders and merchants frequented the city. The largest influx of people to Mecca, however, occurred annually, when warring tribes laid down their weapons and converged upon the city. Agreements among tribal leaders ensured civility, while trade and worship commenced. The

---

67 Jenkins, 57

holy site in the city where many interactions took place centered on the *Ka'aba*, a shrine that contained a sacred black stone. Multiple deities were honored by the various tribes, one of which was a creator deity named *Allah*. The ruling tribe of Mecca over the previous century was the *Quraish*. In approximately 570, one of their own was born, and he was named Muhammad.

Muhammad, whose name means "highly praised," was orphaned early in life. Adopted by his uncle, he spent his youth working as a shepherd tending his uncle's flocks. In his mid-twenties, while working as a merchant, he met a wealthy widow named Khadija and the two of them fell in love. For the next fifteen years, the two are said to have had a very happy marriage, yet he apparently struggled emotionally. It was at this time he began finding solitude in a cave outside of Mecca intent on reflection. One night, known as the first Night of Power, the Angel Gabriel is said to have appeared to him three times and ordered him to proclaim God's message. Transfixed on the message, he was terrified and returned home to his wife, who eventually convinced him of its authenticity and his responsibility to carry out Allah's commands. He agreed with her, and began his ministry. Needless to say, he was initially not a very popular person. He attacked the polytheistic beliefs of the people and their irresponsible lifestyle.[68] The vast majority of people resented the proclamations and resisted change. There was also a clear class hierarchy of citizenry across all tribes, yet Muhammad told them they were all equal in the eyes of the Lord. He had a very small following in the early days of his ministry, and much

---
68   Smith, 227

like Jesus Christ before him was met with intense ridicule. After years of struggle, however, he began to slowly convert more and more people with his message. He soon posed a real political threat to the leaders in Mecca who plotted for his disposal. Fortunately for Muhammad and his followers, the town of Yathrib to the north, seeking political assistance, offered him asylum and the group secretly prepared to move. Assassins scoured the countryside between Mecca and Yathrib making for a perilous journey. This journey has been remembered by history as the *Hijra*.[69] Despite the dangers, the party safely arrived in Yathrib where Muhammad immediately began working in civic administration. As had Jesus and Buddha before him, Muhammad lived a simple life, and was accessible to all comers. Soon Yathrib came to be called Medinat al-Nabi, "the City of the Prophet," or simply Medina.* As welcomed as Muhammad was in Medina, his enemies in Mecca still wanted him dead. Meccan armies attacked Muhammad and the much smaller Medinese forces within two years of Muhammad's arrival in Medina.[70] Despite the overwhelming odds against them, the Meccan army was driven away. Muhammad's forces would grow substantially over a few years and turned on Mecca. Eight years after fleeing the city he returned to conquer it. In an act of leniency unknown in his day, Muhammad forgave his enemies and spared their lives. He was not kind to their religious beliefs, however. He destroyed all evidence of false idols and rededicated the *Ka'aba* to Allah, the one and only God.

The Prophet Muhammad died two years later in 632.

---

69   Smith, 229
  * now it is known as *Medina Monawara*, meaning illuminated city
70   Smith, 230

What had he left to posterity? He was the first to unite all the clans of Arabia, and upon his death, his followers, now known as *Muslims*, or "they who submit to God," controlled nearly the entire Peninsula. But his spiritual message was the true unifying force that resonates to this day for so many people worldwide. The religion, of course is Islam. But what are the base beliefs of those who practice Muhammad's religion? It all starts with the holy book of Islam, the *Qura'an*. Arabic for "recitation," the *Qura'an* is literally the words of God spoken directly to Muhammad.[71] It is distinct from other religious books in that it is written in the first person, the direct words of Allah, spoken in Arabic. It does not translate well into other languages, and the beauty of the words and the flow with which they are expressed cannot be appreciated unless read or recited in Arabic.[72] As Jesus was said to have produced earthly/visible miracles, The Prophet's miracle was his interpretation of the Qura'an. As Houston Smith points out Muhammad proclaimed to his followers:

> *"Do you ask for a greater miracle than this, O unbelieving people, than to have your language chosen as the language of that incomparable Book, one piece of which puts all your golden poetry to shame?"*

The Qura'an was an extension of the Old and New Testaments of the Jewish and Christian faiths for the followers of Muhammad. Like Muhammad as a prophet, it was the final chapter. According to Islam, Abraham, Moses and Jesus were

---

71 Smith, 231
72 Ibid

great prophets among many great prophets, but Muhammad was the "Seal of the Prophets."[73] No prophet will follow him according to their beliefs.

Islamic beliefs are very similar to their Jewish and Christian forerunners, notably in its foundations. Many biblical events are credited as part of the religious history of Islam, with one major difference being the divinity of Jesus Christ. Although Muslims accept the virgin birth of Jesus and the sanctity of the Blessed Mother, to a Muslim is it preposterous to claim God to have had children on earth. Allah is not human, rather other-worldly and awe-inspiring. Allah is all powerful and to be feared by mankind, but is not considered to be ruthless. Quite the contrary he is compassionate and merciful, sympathetic traits which are some of the first words of the *Qura'an*, appearing nearly two-hundred times in total. Immense gratitude to God is expected of all mankind for its creation. Similar to the Christian concept of original sin, *ghaflah*, is when someone forgets his divine origin.[74] Each person must remind himself of the gift of life. So thankfulness or gratitude is the first obligation of a good Muslim. The second goes back to the root meaning of Islam, to completely surrender to Allah, or put another way, be fully committed to his reciprocal love and devotion.[75] Each individual is solely responsible for the eternal soul which he or she is given at birth. According to how people live their lives, at the Day of Judgment souls will pass to heaven or hell. This self-accountability for life's actions and how it relates to eternal salvation is the unifying belief which binds all followers of Islam.[76]

---

73 Smith, 223
74 Smith, 239
75 Smith, 240
76 Smith, 241

Five times daily, Muslims heed a call to prayer. The prayer is called the *Salah*. The Salah starts with reciting two Surahs, one of which is the *Alfatha*, Arabic for "the opening." This is followed by believers bending down while repeating "glorified is my lord, the great!" They then prostrate themselves in reverence of his glory. Finally believers rise from the prostrated position to sit on their knees in prayer. All prayers must be preceded by thorough ritual ablution and are done facing the direction of the holy city of Mecca.[77] Houston Smith translates *Alfatha* the following way:

> *"In the Name of Allah the Merciful, the Compassionate:*
> *Praise be to Allah, Creator of the worlds,*
> *The Merciful, the Compassionate,*
> *Ruler of the Day of Judgment,*
> *Thee do we worship, and Thee do we ask for aid.*
> *Guide us in the straight path,*
> *The path of those on whom Thou hast poured forth*
> *Thy grace.*
> *Not the path of those who have incurred Thy wrath*
> *and gone astray."*

Earlier prophets such as Abraham, Moses and Jesus defined characteristics human beings were expected to live by according to God. Islam takes another step in defining the responsibility of each individual by completing the Five Pillars of its faith. The first is the *Shahadah*, quoted at the outset of this chapter. It is an affirmation of the Muslim reverence for Allah, and something that is expected to be said at least once

---
[77] Smith, 242-243

with conviction in one's life. Muslims are expected to be constant in their devotion to their faith and give to charity. These are the next two pillars, which are self-explanatory, and address general expectations over the course of one's life. The fourth pillar is the observance of Ramadan, which is the same month of the Islamic Calendar that Muhammad received his revelation from the Angel Gabriel and migrated from Mecca to Medina. During Ramadan a follower is expected to not allow anything to pass their lips from sunup to sunset. Once night falls they may partake in moderation. This practice of fasting teaches Muslims the significance of sacrifice and allows them to appreciate the needs of the needy, clearly assisting in their requirement to give to charity. Finally, once in their lifetime they must make a pilgrimage to Mecca if it is physically and economically possible. Meccan pilgrimages require the participants to remove all signs of social status and adorn simple white garments that make all attendees appear equal. This echoes the assertions Muhammad made in reference to equality in the eyes of God.

Following Muhammad's passing, Islamic conquest was swift and decisive. The buffer zone between the warring Sassanian and Byzantine Empires were easy pickings for Muslim armies invading from the south.[78] Within a decade Syria fell, and soon after Jerusalem and Alexandria. By the 8th Century Muslims controlled much of the former territories of Eastern Christianity, North Africa and the Iberian Peninnsula. Only The Frankish King Charles Martel and his army prevented Islamic forces from advancing further into Europe in October 732. Nevertheless, millions of people were now

---

78   MacCulloch, 259-260

under the leadership of powerful militaries united under the flag of a new faith. Many of these people welcomed the new Islamic regimes, who in many cases were more fair and just than the previous Byzantine or Sassanian rulers.[79] The new rulers granted religious freedom to "People of the Book" (Jews and Christians), only persecuting Zoroastrians and other cult religions of the kind.[80] In many cases, like in Syria, matters were seen more in ethnic terms, Syrian or Arab, rather than Muslim or Christian.[81] The Islamic royal courts retained many of the Christian scholars for their own use, and in some cases even Christian clergy.[82] Outside of Arabia, many of the old Christian communities, despite Muslim rule, remained predominately Christian for two or more centuries. There was not a push to convert people or to repopulate areas with Muslims. There was essentially universal karma between all faiths. Eventually, however, things changed. In some cases Christians and Jews were organized into separate 2nd class communities under Muslim protection known as a *dhimma*.[83] Later, some followers of the two faiths were required to wear distinctive clothing in public signifying their lower status in the community.[84] This substandard treatment, along with heavy taxation was likely a major catalyst in the gradual decline in the number of Jewish and Christian residents in the east. Slowly, but steadily, Muslim populations grew. Churches were converted into Mosques and the remaining Christians were forced to

---

79 Jenkins, Philip. *The Lost History of Christianity*. New York: HarperOne, 2008. Print. Pgs., 103-104
80 Ibid
81 Ibid
82 Jenkins, Lost History, 16-17
83 Jenkins, Lost History, 109
84 Ibid

move, convert or endure. The early center of Christianity in the east was now the heart of Islam.

Western thought has historically mistaken Islamic Law on a number of issues. The first is the status of women in the Muslim world. Pre-Islamic Arabia, as earlier mentioned, was an unjust and immoral society which Muhammad was intent on changing. Women were grossly mistreated, and the *Qura'an* forbids such actions. It called for women to be included in inheritance, forbade infanticide and called for overall equality with men in Islamic societies. More importantly it sanctified the bond of marriage. Sex outside the bonds of marriage was forbidden, female consent to a marriage required, and divorce strictly discouraged. Polygyny, having multiple wives, is permitted under certain situations according to Qura'anic Law, yet the practice is not commonplace in much of the Muslim world today. Next, we turn to two Arabic words that stir many western minds with fear and terror; *infidel* and *jihad*. Infidel loosely translates to "one who lacks thankfulness." Remember, everyday Muslims are expected to thank God for life. Jihad is a "struggle," or "exertion." It simply means a religious struggle, and can imply a combative war amongst armies or the war each individual must battle within to find religion and God.[85] The *Qura'an* says "Defend yourself against your enemies, but do not attack them first: God hates the aggressor." The Western world, indeed nearly all of humanity, was traumatized by the tragic events of September 11, 2001. When it became clear Islamic terrorists were behind the attacks, a negative perception of Islam as a whole rooted itself in the west. Sporadic attacks had happened before overseas.

---

85 Smith, 257

Previously, United States Embassies had been attacked, planes had been hijacked and bombs had even exploded on U.S. soil, all the result of Islamic extremists. But something about 9/11 united, in many western minds, all the peaceful Muslims in the world with the terrorists who happened to be followers of the same faith. Perhaps it was western media showing people celebrating in streets in Islamic countries after the towers fell. Or maybe it was the protection Osama Bin Laden, the supposed 9/11 mastermind, received in the mountains by the Afghan warlords that cemented anti-Islamic thought among many. The fact of the matter is the terrorists and those that support them are a small minority in the Muslim world. All countries and all faiths have their extreme factions. Jihads and holy wars against "infidels" spark allusions of terror, but in fact, are reflections on the past when Muslim and Christian armies battled in the Crusades, true holy wars for both sides. Mankind tends to be short-sighted, but we must remember that in the end we are all citizens of planet earth and are all brothers. Islam, like Christianity before it, preaches peace and love. Like a Muslim pilgrimage to Mecca, when they adorn white robes in commonality, all are one in the eyes of god.

Hinduism

"Only that yogi whose joy is inward, Inward his peace, and his vision inward shall come to Brahman......."
Bhagavad-Gita

12,000 years ago ice sheets began to recede all over the globe. The Ice Age had come to an end. The need to scavenge for food for hominids in a frigid landscape gave way to localized foraging for sustenance. Hunter-gatherers far and wide settled down into a pastoral lifestyle. Neolithic settlements emerged everywhere, including the subcontinent of India. By the beginning of the Bronze Age evidence emerged of advanced civilizations. The Harappan was the earliest known civilization that developed in Indus River Valley, beginning in the late 4th Millennia B.C.E. Archaeological discoveries suggest that within a few hundred years the Harappan were as advanced as the Sumerians and Egyptians to the west. Evidence suggests they even engaged in trade with the latter two civilizations.[86] Time passed, and nomadic tribes eventually ventured into India from the Middle East challenging indigenous people. Harappan rule apparently vanished at this time, so it was clearly a period of cultural transition. Scholars debate whether there was definitive worship in ancient India, but few question its development early in the 2nd Century B.C.E. in the northwestern portion of the subcontinent.

The early invaders likely originated In Iran or Afghanistan. Believed to have entered India through the high mountain passes in the northwest, these people were known as The Aryans. Whether they came in large numbers, or streamed in over generations remains debated. What seems almost certain, however, is they brought with them a religious belief system that changed Indian culture forever. They introduced India to *The Vedas*. This collection of accounts was initially passed down verbally for centuries during what is known as the *Vedic Age*, and was not written down until the *Epic Age* much later.[87] * The oldest known texts are the *RigVeda*, and are considered one of the most important collections of documents in Indian history. The RigVeda is a collection of 1,028 hymns called *suktas*, divided into ten books, or *mandalas*. The RigVeda, like the Christian Bible or the Jewish Tanakh, had multiple contributors to its text. It contains an array of information about early Vedic lifestyles and religious practices. Early Indian worship was much like other primitive religions focused on the deification of natural phenomena. Fire, for

---

86 Possehl, Gregory, *The Indus Civilization: A Contemporary Perspective*. Lanham: Altimira Press, 2002. Page 5
87 Bellah, 485 (***composed between 11th-9th Centuries B.C.E.***)
 * Remarkably, the Aryans perfected a system known as hyperorality, which incorporates a complex series of cross-checking for accuracy that kept the stories remarkably accurate. (Bellah 482)

example, was a vital element of early Vedic religious practices and worship of the fire god *Agni* always accompanied rituals.[88] *Indra* was the warrior god, *Soma* the god of an intoxicating drink of the same name. Aryan ancestors in Iran and Afghanistan had worshipped similar gods, and many of the beliefs of the Iranian religion of *Zoroastrianism* mirrored Aryan beliefs.

Eventually, advanced culture spread out from the Indus River Valley into other parts of the subcontinent. The pastoral lifestyle of the Vedic period was slowly being replaced by urban establishments replete with temples and palaces. Image and status became front and center for a population that had drifted away from a more primitive and collective lifestyle. Accompanying this glamorous lifestyle were advances in science and literature which helped build a stronger intellectual base. It was not long before a priestly class developed dedicated to Hindu theology. These priests began posing new questions with respect to the creation of the world. Polytheism slowly began fading into the past as an archaic system of beliefs for Hindus as the idea of a creator god took root. Passages that echo the book of Genesis, in the Old Testament, are seen in the *Nasadiya Sukta* (Hymn of Creation) found in the *RigVeda* (which by this time had finally been inscribed):

> "The all-wise Father saw clearly, and after due reflection created the sky and the earth in their watery form and touching each other. When their boundaries were stretched afar, then the sky and the earth became separated."

---

[88] Bellah, 489-490; 501-502

"At the time death was not, nor immortality; the distinction between day and night was not. There was only One who lived and breathed without the help of air, supported by himself. Nothing was, excepting Him"

"He who has given us life, he who is the Creator, he who knows all the places in this universe-he is one, although he bears the names of many gods."

Other manuscripts were compiled during this period, including the other three *Vedas* (*YajurVeda, SamaVeda* and *AtharvaVeda*). For simplicity's sake I will classify them as ritualistic in nature and pertaining to elements of worship of the *RigVeda*.

A final collection of writings emerged in the late Vedic period, known as the *Upanishads*. The *Upanishads* were tied to the *Vedas* as well, but introduced new philosophies to the Hindu faith. These teachings are known as the *Vedanta* philosophy and lie at the spiritual core of all Hindus. Vedanta teaches human beings to primarily have faith in themselves.[89] Having faith in oneself to the Hindu is having faith in God. Individuals are, in fact, an extension of God and are all divine according to Hindu beliefs. The primary Hindu god, The Supreme Being discussed in the Hymn of Creation, is known as *Brahman*. He is the entire universe and everything in it is part of his being. In other words, everything that exists is simply an extension of Brahman. This theory is a step beyond Christian assertions that God created only man in his image

---
[89] Deluca, David. *Pathways to Joy*. Novato: New World Library, 2003. Print. Pg. 8

and likeness. All living things are Brahman, and Hindus praise all living things. The most sacred animal for the Hindu is the cow. It poses as a symbolic representation of all other animals, and is venerated as a gentle and docile beast. Once again, all living things are Brahman, the cow included. Excerpts from the *Chandogya Upanishad* read as follows:

> "All this is Brahman. Let a man meditate on the visible world as beginning, ending, and breathing in Brahman."

> "He who beholds all beings in the Self, and Self in all beings, he never turns away from it."

> "When, to a man who understands, the Self has become all things, what sorrow, what trouble can there be to him who once beheld that unity."

Our bodies, according to Hindus, are simply outer shells, vessels containing our infinite souls. As Swami Vivekananda explained in the late 19th Century, the human soul is part of the cosmic energy beyond life and death. Your soul was never born, and it will never die. Birth and death belong to the body only, because the soul is eternal.[90] The souls, or *jivas*, are the living *Brahman* within each of us, the *atman*. For the Hindus, indeed for us all in their belief, to reach salvation people must search within themselves and discover this *atman*. *

---

90 Deluca, 6
  * the *jiva* is the soul that transmigrates from one life to the next, whereas *atman* is the Brahman within a person

52 | RELIGION AND MAN

In addition to the development of a priestly class, nobility emerged with advances in civilization. The priests became known as the *Brahmin*, and the nobles and warriors were classified as *Kshatriya*. These two groups represented a very small percentage of the Hindus, however. The common people, artisans and craftsmen were classified as *Vaisya* while servants and unskilled laborers were known as *Sudra*. These were the four *varnas*, India's class system that would endure until modern times. Initially, divisions were loosely formed. Status could be earned or acquired; citizens were not relegated to classification by birth. Eventually, however, the class boundaries solidified. There were strict rules, called *dharmas*, which gave the Brahmins and Kshatriyas many freedoms and also allowed Vaisyas considerable liberties as well. With respect to religion, it was the Sudras who suffered greatly from these rules as they were prohibited from learning or studying the *Vedas*. Without a working knowledge of the proper approach to the Hindu faith, the soul of the Sudra was essentially prevented from eternal salvation with its creator. Fortunately, in their case, the worst case scenario would be rebirth inside another human body in the next life. For Hindus there is no such thing as sin or damnation, because, as previously mentioned, all are part of Brahman, and if God is without sin, and all are part of God, then all are without sin.

One of the remarkable differences in the Hindu faith is their belief in transmigration, or *samsara*. Also known as reincarnation, it begins in basic life forms. As each life ends, the *jiva* within that life form, in theory, advances into the body of a more sophisticated life form. Gradually advancing through multiple, more complex life forms it culminates in a human being. For example, a *jiva* may have begun inside an ant; after the ant dies it passed into a newly hatched dove; then after the bird's death the jiva is transferred to a deer before being reborn inside a human body, perhaps yours. The human body is the final stop for the *jiva* prior to reuniting with *Brahman*. Note, however, one who lives an immoral or evil life may be reborn in another animal, essentially being demoted in the next life. A person may not reach salvation, or *moksa*, in one human lifetime. Your jiva may have been in other humans prior, and destined for others to follow. Only individuals who find Brahman in this life will have their spirit go to him at death. If the wrong actions are taken in life, or in other words if the person does not exhibit proper *karma*, the jiva continue to remain in the cycle of reincarnation.

Now begins each person's quest to uncover his/her *atman*, the inner Brahman within each individual. In Hinduism, there are four paths, or *yogas*, each individual has to choose from in his quest for salvation. Westerners tend to think of *yoga* as solely the physical exercise known as *hatha yoga*, but for Indians it is much more. The four *yogas* are meant to match the four spiritual personalities Hindus believe each person embodies. Individuals, they say, are inclined to be reflective, emotional, active or experimental.

For the reflective person, *Jnana yoga* is the recommended path. When this path is taken, the person must become well-versed in the Hindu scriptures. Once educated, there is intensive reflection and meditation that is expected of the individual. The yogi will soon evolve into experiencing life in the third person. They will consciously disconnect their minds from their bodies, virtually viewing themselves in a spirit form from above. This path clearly requires intensive discipline and attention to detail, not easily traversed.

For the emotional person there is *bhakti yoga*. It is an extremely simplistic path, and one most easily identifiable with the western world. It is a path of love, a wholehearted devotion to Brahman. An active personality may choose *karma yoga*, the working path to salvation. Selfless devotion to all activities, attributing actions to Brahman is the approach of the *karma yogi*.

Finally, for experimental personalities who prefer searching for answers within themselves, there is *raja yoga*. Hindus believe there are four principle layers of each individual; the body, the mind, the inner subconscious and the inner spiritual core. The exercises and meditations of yoga familiar to westerners are the first step the *raja yogi* takes on this path, and the goal is for the mind to reach a point in meditation when it transcends the body and joins with the *atman*. Hindus do not consider the four paths completely exclusive of one another and encourage followers to tailor their own paths to salvation.

Factions eventually emerged, however, with the development of other religions, most notably Buddhism and Jainism. Enter the Indian age of laws and philosophy. Breaking down religious barriers coincided with advances in education for many of the common people. Schools were opened across the land, where compositions, called *sutras*, were compiled. The sutras became the base forms of intellectual enlightenment in India for centuries to follow. Coupling the interplay of the other religions with cross-cultural exchanges, especially in the north, Hindu views were being reshaped. First Persians, and later, Greeks and Romans, interacted with India in warfare and/or trade. The confluence of ideas on multiple fronts was surely a catalyst in a Hindu revival in the first few centuries of the Common Era. Some of the more notable achievements in Indian history in arts, science and literature are attributed to this period, known as the Golden Age of Hinduism.

According to Houston Smith in his book *The World's Religions*, human beings have historically been drawn by three overwhelming desires: pleasure, success and duty.[91] These desires may temporarily fulfill needs, but they really are not the true things people crave. According to the Hindus, what man craves can only be found when sought at the depths of their being.[92] Our real wishes are to have being, knowledge and joy, and we want a limitless supply of all three. In other words, we want to matter, not to simply exist. We search for truths and happiness, not the kind of happiness money and success afford, but internal bliss and contentment. Those things are only attainable by following the Vedanta Philosophy. Vivekananda explained that only the uneducated man looks up to God far away in heaven with trepidation and fear.[93] When, according to their beliefs, God is all around us and we are a part of him. Vivekananda continued by echoing the Gospel of Matthew, "Blessed are the pure in heart, for they shall see God;" Vedanta teaches the same philosophy.

---

[91] Smith, 20
[92] Smith, 21
[93] Deluca, 58

Buddhism

"Decay is inherent in all component things; work out your salvation with diligence"
Dying words of Guatama Buddha

Civilization in India continued to advance in the latter half of the 1st Millennium B.C.E. Colonization of the southern half of the peninsula, south of the Deccan Plateau had begun, while cities and states to the north continued to grow and flourish. The Hindu faith had separated the people by class centuries before, comprising the four *varnas* of *Brahmin*, *Kshatriya*, *Vaisya* and *Sudra*. The *Brahmin* and *Kshatriyas* had subsequently inherited wealth and influence from their ancestors. The *Vaisyas*, too, were afforded wealth and privilege, but most importantly religious freedom of worship. The *Sudras*, however, continued to systematically suffer financially and spiritually as the peasant class. They were not afforded the precious details expected of a devout Hindu to achieve salvation. Thus, in addition to being condemned to a life of poverty, the Sudra would have feared his soul, or *jiva*, would be continuously reincarnated into a life of servitude. Salvation and hope for *Sudras*, however, was on the horizon.

The story of the Great Buddha starts long before his birth. Like their Hindu forefathers, Buddhists believe in samsara (reincarnation). Many lives prior to the birth of the Buddha, his spirit was alive in other early teachers, or *Bodhisattvas*. This spirit was preordained early on to be the "chosen one" that would culminate in the Buddha. In the penultimate life for the spirit, it resided inside a charitable prince named Vessantara, a virtuous and honorable predecessor for the one who was to follow.

On the banks of the Rohini River in the foothills of the Himalayan Mountain Range sat the town of Kapilavatsu. It was the capital of the *Sakya* clan, a small, independent tribal state led by a chief named Suddhodana. In the middle of the 6th Century B.C.E., Suddhodana, who had two wives, had become advanced in age. He lamented as neither of the two wives had borne him a male heir to his throne. One night while lying in bed, the older wife, Maha Maya, dreamed a white elephant entered her womb. The dream bore fruit as nearly a year later she gave birth to a baby boy, naming him Siddhartha Guatama. Suddhodana was overcome with joy and brought in a team of psychics to forecast the boy's future. Nearly all of them agreed that he would be a great leader of his people, but warned if he bore witness to the frailties of life he would turn to the life of a sage.

Guatama was raised in a lifestyle of considerable luxury. He wanted for nothing, and was showered with all of the adoration and affection of a noble of his day. At sixteen, he married a beautiful princess named Yashodhara, and the two later had a son. His father was undoubtedly pleased at the progression of Siddhartha, and probably confident the boy would assume the throne upon his passing. Still, Suddhodana was careful to shelter his son. The premonitions of the psychics still weighed on the old man. Thirteen years passed and Siddhartha, now twenty-nine, wanted to go into the city to explore. His father requested all of the old or sickly be removed from the path of the royal procession. Apparently a few citizens slipped through the cracks. First, the young prince saw an old and decrepit man. A short time later he witnessed a person riddled with disease. Next he saw a corpse. Finally, he saw a sage in intense meditation beneath a tree. At that moment he understood that he had been sheltered from reality. Life was not the pomp and circumstance of the royal court. In fact, it was just the opposite, a cruel evolution into decay. Siddhartha was changed forever. He must have wondered why mankind was given such terrible burdens. He wanted answers to this puzzling dilemma, but realized he would never find the answers living the luxurious lifestyle of a prince. He would have to give up not only his lifestyle, but his family. Certainly it was a difficult choice for Siddhartha, but ultimately, he made his choice. While his wife and young son slept, he slipped away in the middle of the night.

After shaving his head, and trading in his regal attire for that of a pauper, he made off for Rajagriha, the capital city of the Magadha Empire in eastern India. Some Brahman ascetics lived in the hills surrounding the city and Gautama wanted to learn as much about Hindu piety and individual selflessness as he could from these men. He was not satisfied, and after a time departed from their company. He then went away with five disciples and the group began submitting themselves to extraordinary tests of mental and physical endurance with intense fasting and prayer. Again he was not content. He realized he had to find a path in the middle of the extremes of worldly pleasures and the self-mortification of the ascetic.[94] He left his disciples behind and wandered away towards the city of Gaya, on the banks of the Niranjara (Phalgu) River, where he began to meditate beneath a fig tree. It is said he remained there for forty-nine consecutive days and nights, while continuously tormented by the demon Mara. Mara tried to lure him with fleshly pleasures, challenged his mortality as well as his credibility, all to no avail. Eventually the demon realized he could not sway Gautama, so he appealed to Gautama's logic by declaring no one could possibly be intelligent enough to comprehend the profound realities the young sage had discovered. It almost worked. Yet, at length, Gautama replied, "there will be some who understand."[95] Like Jesus Christ would do five centuries later, the temptations of the devil were rejected. Buddha found enlightenment, or *Bodhi*, and was reborn.

Buddha reunited with his five disciples who soon bore witness to his first sermon in the holy town of Benares (present day Varanasi) where Buddha issued the *Four Noble Truths*. First, he explained that life is *dukkha*, or "suffering." The second truth holds that the cause of this suffering is craving, desire or attachment. Buddha was not claiming all life to be suffering, but in accordance to the realization that life is fragile,

---
94 Smith, 85
95 Ibid

and with age comes suffering and death, one's mortality can be depressing.[96] Mankind craves liberation from suffering and disease. Individuals feel physical and emotional pain from personal misery or that of our friends and relatives. Sadly man becomes attached to material possessions or craves the possessions of others. Material cravings have a tendency to torment the mind of individuals. These are the attributes Buddha found to be toxic to the human psyche. This leads to The Third Noble Truth, which states that one must eliminate all of these desires to be content. But how is this achieved? According to Buddha, this is the fourth Noble Truth: one must follow the "Noble Eightfold Path."

The Noble Eightfold Path is essentially training for a good, well-rounded life. Buddha explained that before heading down the path, it is important to be surrounded by individuals that have previously tread the route.[97] This allows the candidate to immediately realize the possibility of success. Once a positive frame of mind is established the journey may begin. The first two steps are goal-oriented. One must have the appropriate views and the right intent from the outset. Clarity provides peace of mind. Of course one has to be wholly committed to the goal. The next four steps are action-oriented. Individuals are expected to speak and conduct themselves with integrity. Unkind words and gossip can be damaging to others as well as one's own character. And with respect to behavior, Buddha echoes the ethical portion of the Ten Commandments: *do not kill; do not steal; do not lie; do not be unchaste; do not consume intoxicants.*[98] A candidate

---

96 Bellah, 532
97 Smith, 104-105
98 Smith, 107-108

should have a reputable profession that is not self-damaging or damaging to others. And in said profession, the right effort is expected for success and happiness. The final two steps of the path are mind-oriented. The first is mindfulness, or awareness. In the Buddhist case, this means intense mindfulness of the tiniest details, of every action of every day. This ultra-keen awareness awakens the spirit and alerts the mind of all surrounding actions. This is achieved by the last step, intense concentration, as found in raja yoga. According to Buddha, this is the path to enlightenment.

When one achieves Bodhi (enlightenment), he is said to have reached *nirvana*. This is the pinnacle for the Buddhist follower, the apex of the human spirit. Translated as "extinguished," or "blown out," nirvana is the complete obliteration of all the bonds of humanity.[99] Buddha explained that nirvana is incomprehensible for the human mind to fathom, and when pressed for an explanation, he simply replied that it would be sheer and utter "bliss."[100] Buddha did not believe in a conventionally defined creator God, yet he did not deny creation either. The "creator" is not defined, and like nirvana itself, is indescribable. Nirvana and God are essentially one in the same in Buddhism.

As far as what Buddhists believe in regards to an afterlife, it gets complicated. Buddhists, like their Hindu forefathers, believe in samsara (reincarnation). The Buddha, however, did not believe human beings have souls. Hinduism, which laid the foundation for Buddhism, certainly maintains the belief of a soul, so how could The Buddha have been so distinctly

---
99 Smith, 113
100 Ibid

different from his root faith? For the Hindu, the soul is a spiritual substance that retains an eternal identity as it passes through successive lives. As described above, to attain nirvana is to dispose of all human bonds. Man exists in boundaries, from their bodies and their minds to their existence on earth in a small corner of the universe. And in human existence, everything is always changing and evolving in time and space. In other words, nothing is static or permanent in the universe. This constant impermanence Buddha called *anicca*.[101] So, Buddhists believe, at death each person that has not reached enlightenment will have the remnants of their "being" go back into the great abyss, a melting pot if you will, where parts of their spirit will be reincarnated in future lives.[102] But just as in Hinduism, those that do reach enlightenment, or nirvana, will not be put back into the mix, they will join the infinite, boundless existence of the great unknown.

Buddha and his followers spent approximately forty-five years traveling throughout northeastern India converting thousands of people to Buddhist teachings. At one point he returned to Kapilavatsu at the request of his elderly father. Ostensibly, his father hoped to convince his son to return to the Sakya Clan and govern the people. Gautama had other ideas. Not only did Buddha not return to stay, he converted his still-faithful wife and his young son to his cause. Ultimately, his destiny was not of this world. Sometime in what many regard as his 80th year, Buddha ate a tainted meal and died of a food-borne illness. With many of his followers looking on, he found Nirvana.

---

101 Smith, 117
102 Ibid

Buddha never intended to invent a new religion and viewed himself as a Hindu reformer. He saw fundamental flaws in the old Hindu system and wanted it overhauled. Nevertheless, a new religion was born under Gautama. According to Houston Smith, there are six aspects that can be found in nearly all religions in history; authority, ritual, speculation, tradition, grace and mystery.[103] Much of what we looked at in the first chapter touched on these aspects. Nearly all religions begin with a leader or leaders championing some form of ritual. The ritual may lead to speculation about the nature of the ritual and what it means for the participants. Questions surrounding the meaning of existence arise, leading to the development of religious beliefs, and traditions emerge. The human mind cannot fathom infinity, so the details remain a mystery, but the saving grace for many is the belief they are taken care of by a higher power. Amazingly, Buddhism contains virtually none of these six aspects at its core.[104] The Brahmin authority that controlled the Hindu faith kept the poor from religious worship. For the ones who were receiving instruction, Buddha challenged them to think for themselves instead of blindly accepting the teachings of the time. He viewed ritual as pointless, and to speculate on the unknown was considered a waste of time. He believed Hindu traditions hindered the growth of individuals, and that each person is responsible for their own spiritual development.[105] Buddha believed there was no saving grace of an almighty being for his followers, thus there was no mystery of the supernatural. Buddhist beliefs hold

---

103 Smith, 92-93
104 Smith, 94
105 Smith, 96

that everything leading to enlightenment is present in one's own mind.

In nearly all religions throughout history, there were dissentions that often resulted in division. Buddhism proved to be no different. One branch, *Theravada Buddhism*, embraced individual worship and selfless devotion. That branch believes there is no divine help in the quest for nirvana. Theravada, which means the "Way of the Elders," claims to be the purest form of Buddhist worship. It is the path which focuses on less ritual, but intense meditation, and is the one most commonly associated with the priestly class/monks in Buddhism. *Mahayana Buddhism* on the contrary contends there is a celestial force that steers followers to the right path. The Mahayana sect focuses on communal worship, much more ritual and less meditation. This is a less arduous path for Buddhists, and as such, is often preferred by the lay person as evidenced by the fact that Mahayana is practiced by the majority of Buddhists in Asia.

China

"If there is righteousness in the heart, there will be beauty in the character. If there is beauty in the character, there will be harmony in the home. If there is harmony in the home, there will be order in the nation. If there is order in the nation, there will be peace in the world"

Confucius

Ancient China was at war. The *Zhou Dynasty*, which had controlled China since the end of the 2nd Millennium B.C.E., had slowly lost its grip on power. Vast swaths of land that began as sparsely populated fiefdoms had gradually become urbanized. Larger population densities fueled dissention, and widespread warfare erupted. This type of violence was not typical under earlier Zhou rule. Established in approximately 1045 B.C.E. following the collapse of the *Shang Dynasty*, principles were central to the Zhou's core foundations. Claiming to have the Mandate of Heaven, or divine blessing, the Zhou thought a higher power had the ability to remove rulers who behaved in an immoral or unethical manner. They were the fortunate beneficiaries of the Shang losing this mandate. The ancient Chinese believed heaven *(tian)* was an extension of their physical existence on earth, and the two maintained a symbiotic relationship. Consisting of their ancestors *(ti)*, and ruled by a supreme ancestor *(Shang Ti)*, heaven dictated much of the welfare of the living. To return favor, sacrifices were performed for the heavenly ancestors for appeasement and fortune. Ritual was thus a vital element in early Chinese religious proceedings. It extended to the battlefield, where ceremonial offerings were made to ancestors for divine blessing while in combat. Chivalry was the norm, as the invading army was often given gifts prior to battle. Soldiers socialized with one another, even traded weapons prior to the fight. Battles were nearly always fought over honor and prestige, rarely because of greed or fortune. It would all change.

In 771 B.C.E., the Zhou capital was attacked by barbarian hordes and the aristocracy fled east, reestablishing the regime in the town of Louyang. From that point on, Zhou imperial leadership was effectively ceremonial. As populations grew, familiarity amongst rival groups waned. No longer was honor and respect common amongst combatants, rather these traits were replaced with wholesale savagery. Mass slaughters of men, women and children became commonplace following conquests. Houston Smith mentions one case where captives were thrown into boiling cauldrons and their relatives forced to eat the human soup.[106] Morality in China had clearly lost its way.

---

106 Smith, 160

In approximately 551 B.C.E., in present day eastern China, halfway to Beijing from Shanghai as the crow flies, a child was born to a poor family. The child, a boy, named Confucius, had an unspectacular childhood, before devoting himself to education as a young man. He focused on the resurrection of morality in his country, a return to early Zhou principles. He wanted a leadership role in government in order to implement his ideas into law, but he was never allowed to ascend to levels of power. His peers simply feared his popularity was too great. Confucius, to his dismay, was relegated to teacher and advisor for the remainder of his life. Much of his adulthood was spent roaming through various territories looking to advise governments on the proper methods of rule. Unfortunately, his advice routinely fell on deaf ears. He was mocked and taunted for his persistence. Eventually he would return to his home state where he lived out his years, dying at the age of seventy-two. Only after his death did his legend grow, and his lessons impacted China forever.

Confucius left his followers with simple concepts for living life and his ideas have polarized humanity ever since. He believed that to return to the values exhibited by his ancestors, families must turn inward, focusing on themselves. Moral foundations should be ingrained in children from their parents, and passed down from generation to generation. In modern times this is an assumed fact of life, but in his time it clearly was not. For Confucius, the duty of his country was to focus on the living, not the dead. Chinese worship had become too fixated on ancestral homage. In the meantime, life on earth had become a struggle for the living. Confucius felt it was time to reverse the trend. As Confucius said when asked about death, he replied, "You do not understand even life. How can you understand death?"[107]

Humanity was at the heart of Confucius' teachings. The "golden rule" many are familiar with was one of his principles. The golden rule is the basis for the attribute known as *jen*. Jen was the ultimate virtue for Confucius. Defined as mutual self-respect and a compassionate love for others, jen was considered the perfect relationship between people. *Chun Tsu* was equally important in Confucius' mind. Chun Tsu is the charisma of the good natured person who embraces jen. The two terms essentially go hand-in-hand.

Li, is the third Confucian principle, and it is defined as propriety, or the way things should be done. This concept is divided into five categories: The Rectification of Names, the Doctrine of the Mean, the Five Great Relationships, the Regard for Age and Regard for Family. The first regards simple semantics. For Confucius, it was important for everything to have an appropriate/descriptive name to avoid confusion in society. If you were a king, you should have the proper title, a merchant likewise. It seems rather trivial, but properly suited descriptive nouns were likely not as common in Ancient China as in today's world. As far as the Doctrine of the Mean, it issued a commonly held principle to have nothing in excess, everything in moderation. The Five Great Relationships are those between a parent and child, husband and wife, two siblings, two friends and a ruler and his subject. Confucius argued that each person should act in accordance with his position to maintain balance. The subject should know his place with respect to the ruler, the child to the parent, and so on.

---
107 Smith, 185

Finally Confucius proclaimed that the elderly should be venerated and cared for by the young and the family respected as the ultimate institution of society. The importance of family to Confucius has already been noted. As far as the care for the elderly, it was a way for young people to "pay it forward," but it also helped preserve the wisdom and knowledge older people gain with time. The elderly were tremendously valuable in the eyes of Confucius, and an integral part of every family.

What of the responsibility of the ruling class? For Confucius a just ruler, one who exhibits *Te*, enjoys the will of the people.[108] This head of state must possess a selfless approach to effective rule. Oppressive leaders will lose the people, and eventually the throne. When one ruler asked Confucius his stance on capital punishment, Confucius responded:

> *What need is there of the death penalty in government? If you showed a sincere desire to be good, your people would likewise be good. The virtue of the prince is like the wind; the virtue of the people like grass. It is the nature of grass to bend when the wind blows it.*[109]

The final core concept for Confucius was *wen*, or simply, the arts. Poetry, music, arts, philosophy, et.al, raises culture to a greater plateau for Confucius.   Wen was education, and for Confucius the educated were more prudent in the course of their lives.

Confucianism is a social belief system. Quite the contrast

---

108 Smith, 178
109 Smith, 179

with *Buddhism*, Confucius professed that human interaction was central for a happy existence on earth. It is in this life he wanted his followers to focus their efforts on, not a confounding afterlife. In this respect they have commonality with Buddhist views. For Confucius, self-cultivation was a constant practice, that when refined was perfection. Each individual has their own responsibility for the collective well-being of society. *Confucianism* was not the only belief system prevalent in China at the time. The Mohist philosophy was a popular movement, along with Yangism from the philosopher Yang Zhu. The most enduring, however, came from a mysterious figure from the west.

Lao Tzu, if he really lived, was a royal archivist of the Zhou. Some experts date his life to before that of Confucius. Others claim he lived at a later period. There are assertions his mother was impregnated while observing a shooting star, that he remained in her womb for over sixty years, and when born emerged old and grey. He lived a reclusive life until a very old age, and eventually became frustrated with society. Mounting a water buffalo, he rode away to retire in complete obscurity, but before he departed left a brief explanation of his views for mankind. He had no disciples and it is believed he did not preach or teach. Yet he is credited with founding one of the more important faiths in human history.

Lao Tzu introduced China to *Daoism*, or "the way." The *Daodejing* was the short manual he inscribed before riding away on a water buffalo for eternity. The *Daodejing*, along with the *Zhuangzi* (which was composed later) comprise the two central volumes of Daoist beliefs. Daoist beliefs have crisscrossed Confucian ideals from the beginning. Confucians, on one hand, wanted to change society by bringing morality back to the leaders. Daoists, on the other hand, wanted to distance themselves from government. The *Dao* principle of *wuwei* is this hands-off approach to all aspects of life. It is an approach that suggests human intervention creates unnecessary friction that interferes with the normal flow of nature. Thus, Daoists suggest letting nature run its own course. The higher power ruling the cosmos will "take care" of things.

Dao (the way) is difficult to explain in words. It is beyond human comprehension. Yet it surrounds all of humanity according to its followers. Human beings are a part of the *Dao* before birth and after death, and are within the *Dao* during life.[110] The driving force of the *Dao* is *Te*, or its power. Individuals have their own supply of *Te*, as it is the essence of life. There are three separate divisions of Daoism. Religious Daoists, more closely associated with the *Dao Chiao*, (Daoist Church) focus on mystic rituals performed by priests or shamans that assist in summoning divine powers from the spirits, or the *shen*. Vitality Daoists, in turn, look to increase their supply of *Te*. These followers experience *ch'i or Qi,* which is the *Te* flowing through their bodies. They look to increase the supply and flow of vital energy with matter, movement and their minds.[111] The matter comes in the form of food, drink or medicinal herbs that may be consumed. Examples can be seen at any Chinese pharmacy with its vast array of medicinal herbs. Movement comes in forms such as dance, calisthenics, and martial arts. Yoga taps into the mind for these individuals. They believe meditation empties the mind which allows the

---

110 Bellah, 447
111 Smith, 201

Te to readily flow into the body. Meditation enhances the vital essence of *ch'i*, known as the *jing*. Arthur Waley portrayed Daoist beliefs in the following way:

> *It is close at hand, stands indeed at our very side; yet is intangible, a thing that by reaching for cannot be got. Remote it seems as the farthest limit of the Infinite. Yet it is not far off; every day we use its power. For the Way of the Vital Spirit fills our whole frames, yet man cannot keep track of it. It goes, yet has not departed. It comes, yet is not here. It is muted, makes no note that can be heard, yet all of a sudden we find that it is there in the mind. It is dim and dark, showing no outward form, yet in a great stream it flowed into us at our birth.*[112]

Philosophical Daoists comprise the third group. *Tao* is like water, always flowing, constantly changing. This was a parallel early Taoists embraced. They believed the proper way to live life is to ride the wave of the *Tao*. Individuals should surrender themselves to what is a greater power. In this way the person lives their life to the fullest, maximizing *Te*. Revisiting the concept of *wuwei*, the Philosophical Daoist seeks to preserve their energy, not waste it on unnecessary activities. These individuals want everything to be accomplished with maximum efficiency. Even great feats should be accomplished with little exertion.

Daoists frown on selfishness, embracing selflessness. They shun aggression. Individual ambition is not acceptable

---

[112] Waley, Arthur. *The Way and Its Power*, New York: Grove Press, 1958. 48-49

in their beliefs. The natural world in all its beauty is truly appreciated by the devout. This devotion to nature is evident in the arts and the architecture of ancient China. The balance of Daoism lies at the heart of the faith. This balance is identified in the principles of the *yin* and the *yang*. Everything in the world is polarized with its counterpart: positive/negative, male/female, good/evil, day/night, etc. Everything is cyclical in Daoism, constantly revolving back to itself.

Confucianism and *Daoism* were born in the *Axial Age* in China and, like the *yin* and *yang*, have complemented one another from the beginning. Confucius wanted to change the morality of China, whereas Lao Tzu wished to avoid conflict altogether. Confucius asked for a proactive approach to life. Lao Tzu was reclusive, stressed to his followers to "go with the flow." Both faiths would prove crucial in shaping the future of China.

Reflections

"That which is impenetrable to us really exists. Behind the secrets of nature remains something subtle, intangible, and inexplicable. Veneration for this force beyond anything that we can comprehend is my religion."

Albert Einstein

The diversity of earth's inhabitants mirrors the diversity of its faiths. There are thousands of active religions and countless deceased belief systems. This book has reviewed the major faiths, which with the inclusion of atheists/non-religious beliefs, comprise over 90% of the dogmas of the human race. Humanity wants to believe it exists for a reason. Anything that undermines these beliefs is met with resistance. Look no further than the Catholic Church which persecuted Galileo Galilei for advocating a heliocentric solar system. The Vatican vehemently condemned such "heresy" of the day and Galileo was ultimately condemned to house arrest for the remainder of his life. But why would a scientific theory such as Galilei's be so damning in the eyes of the Vatican? Put simply, it diminished human importance. The Catholic Church was defending the subconscious wall humanity has put up from its beginnings. To advocate the sun was the center of the solar system diminished the importance of the home planet of mankind, or the "chosen ones." For Galileo, however, he was just touching the tip of the iceberg. If the Vatican was intimidated by his "radical" notions in the 17th Century, it would likely convulse over the scientific knowledge mankind has acquired in just the last century.

Can mankind be insignificant? Is it blasphemous to assert such a claim? It seems a bit unlikely that our race is completely insignificant. Still, it seems equally unlikely that it's special or extraordinary. The magnitude of the universe is as unfathomable as the concept of infinity, or God if you will. Our solar system is located in one spiral arm of the Milky Way galaxy. The solar system contains one star (our sun) in a galaxy of upwards of 400 billion other stars. The Milky Way alone is over 100,000 light years in diameter.[113] The scale is already massive. It's about to get really confounding. The nearest large galaxy to the Milky Way is the Andromeda Galaxy, a "mere" 2.3 million light years away from earth. The Milky Way and Andromeda Galaxies are in a cluster of galaxies called the Local Group which contains over fifty galaxies alone, each one containing billions of stars. The Local Group and over one hundred other clusters of galaxies are in the Virgo Supercluster of galaxies that span an estimated 110

---

113 Light speed over 186,000 miles per second......fastest thing in universe in theory

million light years. The Virgo Supercluster is one of millions of superclusters of galaxies that populate a universe that is between 13-5 and 17 billion light years in diameter. Pause, for a moment, and ponder the magnitude of scale. The Milky Way contains 400 billion stars. It is one of roughly fifty galaxies in the Local Group, each galaxy roughly 2 million light years apart, containing approximately 400 billion stars. Then the Local Group is part of the Virgo Supercluster, one of millions of superclusters spanning the universe. It is simply impossible to fathom.

The magnitude of the universe we reside in is clearly beyond human comprehension. Steven Weinberg, a Nobel Prize winning physicist wrote the following:

> *However all these problems may be resolved, and whichever cosmological model proves correct, there is not much comfort in any of this. It is almost irresistible for humans to believe we have some special relation to the universe, that human life is not just a more-or-less farcical outcome of a chain of accidents reaching back to the first three minutes, but that we were somehow built in from the beginning.....It is hard to realize that this [earth] is just a tiny part of an overwhelmingly hostile universe. It is even harder to realize that the present universe has evolved from an unspeakably unfamiliar early condition, and faces a future extinction of endless cold or intolerable heat. The more the universe seems comprehensible, the more it seems pointless.*[114]

---
114 Bellah, 54

Well-known scientist Michio Kaku once compared human comprehension of the observable universe to fish swimming in a body of water. The fish may be able to see the surrounding landscape immediately outside its own body of water or "universe" yet cannot comprehend what is beyond. The fish has no idea that it resides in a body of water, on planet earth, inside a small solar system, etc., etc. Mankind may well be as ignorant. We can only see what is in our own proverbial bubble. There may be other bubbles or universes surrounding our own. Weinberg, as well as Stephen Hawking supports the belief that there are multiple universes. Clearly no current technology can give any definitive answer either way.

Humanity, in many ways, has long played a guessing game. Philip Jenkins in *The Lost History of Christianity* quoted a dialogue between the 8th Century bishop Timothy and his Muslim caliph Al-Mahdi :

> *Imagine we are all in a dark house in the middle of the night. If, at night and in a dark house, a precious pearl happens to fall in the midst of people, and all become aware of its existence, everyone would strive to pick up the pearl, which will not fall to the lot of all but to the lot of one only, while one will get hold of the pearl itself, another one of a piece of glass, a third one of a stone or of a bit of earth, but everyone will be happy and proud that he is the real possessor of the pearl. When, however, night and darkness disappear, and light and day arise, then every one of those people who had believed that they had the pearl, would extend and stretch their hand towards the light, which*

alone can show what everyone has in hand. The one who possesses the pearl will rejoice and be happy and pleased with it, while those who had in hand pieces of glass and bits of stone only will weep and be sad, and will sigh and shed tears.[115]

Clearly alluding to religion, it may be possible that one of the world's faiths possesses the "pearl of truth." It is also possible the truth is not known. Mankind remains shrouded in mystery concerning the matter.

Imagine a mountain with a bounty of food at its peak. Surrounding the base are famished multitudes eager to climb the summit and eat their fill. They congregate into smaller, organized groups and plot their own, individual paths to the top. Each group feels its path is the most accurate and successful, and all parties depart the foothills in hopes of scaling the mountain. Ultimately, all groups successfully make the ascent. All paths proved to be true. In September of 1893, a grand conclave was held in Chicago, Illinois. It was the world's first Parliament of Religions, where representatives of numerous faiths gathered to share their respective beliefs. Swami Vivikananda was the delegate representing the Hindu faith. I will conclude the book with an excerpt of his remarks at the convention:

It fills my heart with joy unspeakable to rise in response to the grand words of welcome given to us by you. I thank you in the name of the most ancient

---
115 Jenkins: *The Lost History of Christianity*. Page 17

order of monks the world has ever seen, of which the Buddha was only a member. I thank you in the name of the Mother of religions, of which Buddhism and Jainism are but branches; and I thank you, finally in the name of the millions and millions of Hindu people....I am proud to belong to a religion that has taught the world both tolerance and universal acceptance....We believe not only in universal tolerance but we accept all religions to be true. I will quote to you, sisters and brothers, a few lines from a hymn which every Hindu child repeats every day. I feel that the very spirit of this hymn, which I have repeated from my earliest boyhood, which is every day repeated by millions and millions of people in India, has at least come to be realized. "As the different streams, having their sources in different places, all mingle their water in the sea; O Lord, so the different paths which men take through different tendencies, various though they appear, crooked or straight, all lead to Thee."[116]

---

116 Deluca, 254